Claustrophobia

Ikon Gallery	**6 June - 2 August 1998**
Middlesbrough Art Gallery	15 August - 10 October 1998
Mappin Art Gallery, Sheffield	23 January - 14 March 1999
Dundee Contemporary Arts	27 March - 9 May 1999
Cartwright Hall, Bradford	15 May - 8 August 1999
Aberystwyth Arts Centre	September - October 1999
Centre for Visual Arts, Cardiff	November 1999 - January 2000

Howard Arkley

Uta Barth

Mark Bennett

James Casebere

Mat Collishaw

Carolyn Eskdale

Melanie Friend

Mona Hatoum

Permindar Kaur

Matthias Müller

Nina Saunders

Doris Salcedo

Kathy Temin

Meyer Vaisman

Carrie Mae Weems

Rachel Whiteread

"The unmaking of civilisation inevitably requires a return to and mutilation of the domestic, the ground of all making."

Elaine Scarry, *The Body in Pain*, Oxford University Press, 1985

Claustrophobia

Foreword

Claustrophobia marks the first group exhibition in the galleries
of the new Ikon. Conceived during a time of transition and
rehousing for Ikon itself, it developed from an enquiry into
the prominence of the domestic in the work of contemporary
artists in the 1990s. What emerged was a selection of works
by artists from Australia, North and South America and
Europe, which, when brought together for the first time, could
create intriguing pathways through the accoutrements of home.

The model of the group exhibition has undergone
transformations and mutations over the past two decades.
With the rise of the 'curated' exhibition, there has been a
danger of fitting art into the straitjacket of the curatorial
concept. Claustrophobia attempts to provide the opportunity
for artists, participants and visitors to respond to a range of
work through a theme which aims to open up ideas rather than
restrict or close down meaning. It offers explorations through
the familiar to other worlds - perhaps those of dreams or even
those of nightmares. Whilst each of the works retains its own
character and makes its own impact on the individual, the
correlation of works together in the spaces of the galleries
here at Ikon, and at each of the six tour venues across the UK
until the year 2000, creates contexts which give rise to new
understandings of the work of sixteen very different artists.

These new stories would not have materialised without the
enthusiastic response of the artists to the initial proposal and
their inspired contributions and thoughts on the inclusion of

specific works. We would like to thank in particular the five artists who were commissioned to produce new works for the exhibition, for their extraordinary commitment to the project - Uta Barth, Carolyn Eskdale, Permindar Kaur, Nina Saunders and Meyer Vaisman - and in addition, those artists who have remade or reformed existing works. Our thanks must also go to the artists' representatives for their assistance, the collections for the loan of works over such an extended period of time and the financial support of the Henry Moore Foundation and the Australia Council which enabled the creation of stunning new pieces and installations. The development of this project would not have been possible without a research and development grant from the Arts Council of England and Professional Development International Exchange Programme Award to Australia from the British Council in 1996.

This catalogue presents a collection of voices and ideas across fiction, social-documentary, psychoanalysis, philosophy, poetry and art criticism. The commissioned writers Saskia Beudel, Yvette Brackman, Julian Holder, Lisa Jardine, Soo Jin Kim and Patricia Newell present their responses to new works in progress as we go to press. What emerges is a catalogue and exhibition which are neither the last word nor a return home, but rather journeys back and forth, through the places and locations of home, across the globe and in our minds.

Elizabeth A. Macgregor
Director

Claire Doherty
Curator

"It is stripped off - the paper - in great patches all around the head of my bed, about as far as I can reach and in a great place on the other side of the room low down. I never saw a worse paper in my life. One of those sprawling flamboyant patterns committing every artistic sin. It is dull enough to confuse the eye in following, pronounced enough, to constantly irritate and provoke study, and when you follow the lame uncertain curves for a little distance they suddenly commit suicide - plunge off at outrageous angles, destroy themselves in unheard of contradictions... Through watching so much at night, when it changes so. I have finally found out. The front pattern does move - and no wonder! The woman behind shakes it! Sometimes I think there are a great many women behind, and sometimes only one, and she crawls around fast, and her crawling shakes it all over. Then in the very bright spots she keeps still, and in the very shaky spots she just takes hold of the bars and shakes them hard. And she is all the time trying to climb through. But nobody could climb through that pattern - it strangles so; I think that is why it has so many heads. They get through and then the pattern strangles them off and turns them upside down, and makes their eyes white!"

Charlotte Perkins Gilman, *The Yellow Wallpaper*, Virago, 1996 (first published in 1892), p. 13 and p. 30

Claustrophobia

We're not in Kansas anymore...

GLINDA: What have your learned?
DOROTHY: If I ever go looking for my heart's desire again,
I won't look further than my own back yard. And if it isn't there,
I never really lost it to begin with. Is that right?
GLINDA: That's all it is. And now those magic slippers will take you
home in two seconds,
...Close your eyes...click your heels together three times...
and think to yourself...there's no place like home...

"The Wizard of Oz", that seemingly transparent tribute of
mass appeal to the primacy of "home" over "away", has been
alternatively cast by writer Salman Rushdie as a paean of
the imaginative powers of the exile, to the creation of Oz
"anywhere, and everywhere, except the place from which we
began."[1] It is a film centred around a rite of passage through
the tropes of knowledge (a brain), emotional maturity (a heart)
and strength (courage), but for which the central quest and
ultimate trophy is home.

As Dorothy emerges from the monochrome, mid-western
existence of Kansas into the blinding technicolor of Oz, she is
homeless. As Rushdie has indicated, "her homelessness, her
unhousing, is underlined by the fact that, after all the door-play
of the transitional sequence, and having now stepped out of
doors, she will not be permitted to enter any interior at all
until she arrives at the Emerald City. From Tornado to
Wizard, Dorothy never has a roof over her head."[2]

Watching the full 101 minutes, now 60 years after its
release in the summer of 1939, I was struck by the visual
impact of one of the key tools of the initial narrative - the
house - the vehicle for Dorothy's journey, the weapon of
her destruction of evil and the site of her reawakening. In

Wizard of Oz
BFI Films: Stills, Posters and Designs
Courtesy: Warner Bros

hindsight, this emblem of transition, triumph and security could
not have been a more apt metaphor for "the heart's desire"
at a moment when the world teetered on the edge of chaos,
displacement and loss, engendered by the outbreak of World
War II.

In the late 1990s, at the threshold of the new Millennium
(to whatever extent a marketed construct that may be), in
a context of nostalgia, reassessment and hope, so it seems
that the sign of home - the domestic - is once again achieving
cultural prominence. Whilst socially and economically, Britain
is still coming to terms with the legacy of Thatcherism,
particularly the impact of housing policies and "right-to-buy
incentives", the shifts in domestic policy are not about to
result in a socialist embracement of anti-consumerism. "Cool
Britannia" is designed by Conran and furnished by IKEA.

Signs are that the population is embracing this vision of
"Lifestyle Britain", revealed in the high viewing figures for TV
shows such as "Home Front" and "Changing Rooms", promoted
from the mediocrity of Daytime TV to Prime Time. So too
the Ideal Home Exhibitions in London and Birmingham in 1998
achieved record attendance of over half a million visitors each.
The most dynamic growth area in consumer magazines since
the Male Interest ("Loaded") genre is currently recognised in
the trade as homes and interiors.[3]

What has emerged is not a revisionist fifties' passion for
consumer goods, but rather a desire for immediate histories,
communicated through the domestic - for homes that appear
to display the experiences and events of a "life less ordinary".
House and furnishings have become more readily consumed

1 Salman Rushdie,
"A Short Text About
Magic", The Wizard of
Oz, BFI Film Classics,
1992, p. 57
2 Ibid. p. 33
3 Source: IPC
Magazines, London

left
Robbin Schiff, *Nightmare Bathroom*
mixed media site installation at Womanhouse, 1972

below right
Sandy Orgel, *Linen Closet*
mixed media site installation at Womanhouse, 1972

analogues for constructed identities, which can be discarded at will. As Nikos Papastergiadis has suggested, "the only difference between the traditional and the modern home is that the former was always seen as a complete container of memories and a stable site of identification, whereas the latter is more a patchwork of silent ambitions and temporary arrangements. John Berger hints at the unstated dreams and unstable ground in modernity where he states that "home is no longer a dwelling but the untold story of a life being lived."[4]

Some may conclude that we are returning to the home in the 1990s as a narcissistic withdrawal from post-modernity into a seemingly controllable and secure domestic cocoon. For women historically, of course, the domestic has always been identified with a lived reality. It is neither a retreat nor a segregated zone from the business of life. But the search for stability, for the ideal home, still generates repression and disillusionment, as well as sales figures. In 1991, repossessions reached their peak, shattering the home ownership dream. Campaigning by groups such as Shelter has continued to highlight the lack of investment in permanent affordable homes.[5] The luxury of a domestic cocoon should not be under-estimated, but the compulsion for it also reveals as much about the zeitgeist, about the body politic, as it does about private ambitions and dreams.

In the late 20th Century, the home has thus become transitory, rapidly formed and rapidly reworked in new localities. As Nancy Spector has suggested, the ideal home, fashioned over decades of cultural formation, is carried with us throughout our adult lives, against which the present is enacted.[6] Home is both a fiction, generated by mass media and cultural stereotypes, and a lived reality; the two are co-dependent and generate the psychic constant which is the root of our identities.

4 Nikos Papastergiadias, "The home in modernity", inIVA publications 02, 1997
5 Source: 30 Years of Shelter, brochure 1996
6 Nancy Spector, "Robert Gober: Homeward - Bound", Parkett 27, 1991, pp. 80-88

If then, as Papastergiadis has suggested, "irrespective of its location, the home is the sacred place from which everything else is mapped"[7], the domestic reveals itself as one of the most powerful metaphors for our existence on the cusp of another millennium. Not surprisingly it has proved one of the key focuses and inspirations for contemporary artists, though the histories of its use and transformation are by no means confined to the 1990s.

The domestic in visual art has historically been essentialised as feminine. It was the Other against which modernist art and architecture were defined. Le Corbusier, for example, criticised the "sentimental hysteria that surrounds the cult of the house".[8] Critically current works of art which employ the domestic have been legitimated by a cast of male forebears - Joseph Beuys, Robert Smithson, Richard Hamilton and Vito Acconci amongst others - but rarely is reference made to the cultural heritage of feminism.

In 1972, a condemned mansion in Los Angeles became "Womanhouse", a collaborative art environment. Created by twenty-one students in the Feminist Art Program at the California Institute of the Arts, under the direction of artists Judy Chicago and Miriam Schapiro, it has been described as "a walk-in rumination on the condition of women's lives."[9] The transformed mansion literally embodied the collaborative and consciousness-raising objectives of the early Feminist Art Movement. The series of seventeen rooms revealed the problematic of an essentialist view of the feminine as identified with the domestic interior. Sandy Orgel's "Linen Closet", was described by one woman visitor as symbolising exactly where women have always been, "between the sheets and on the shelf"; whilst in Robbin Schiff's "Nightmare Bathroom" the female body literally dissolved into the substance of the bath, representing the psychological dissolution of female identity into the categories of house-wife/mother/sister/daughter.

"Womanhouse" is recognisably of the period - the literal translation of the political objectives of resistance and

7 Papastergiadias, op. cit.
8 Le Corbusier, Towards a New Architecture, trans. Frederick Etchells, 1927, New York: Prager, 1960
9 Sharon Haar and Christopher Reed, "Coming Home: A Postscript on Postmodernism", Not at Home: The Suppression of Domesticity in Modern Art and Architecture, Thames & Hudson, 1996, p. 255. Womanhouse was opened to the public between 30 January and 28 February 1972 and attracted 10,000 visitors.

reform into art works. Its counterpart in Britain, "Housework" located in Lambeth in 1975, comprised of much the same type of interventionist and collaborative practice.[10] Since the 1970s, North America has seen the institutionalisation of such practices in a range of curated survey exhibitions; from "Out of the House" at the Whitney Museum of Art, New York, (1978), "The House that Art Built" at the Main Art Gallery, California State University in Fullerton and "At Home", curated by Arlene Raven, at Long Beach Museum of Art, California (1983) to "House Rules" at the Wexner Center for the Arts, Columbus, Ohio (1994), "No Place Like Home" at the Walker Art Center, Minneapolis (1997) and perhaps the least overtly politically engaged "Pleasures and Terrors of Domestic Comfort" at the Museum of Modern Art, New York (1991). In Britain, institutions have rarely surveyed such work, preferring to reflect individual responses to the subject such as the work of Rachel Whiteread, Marina Abramovic, Robert Gober and Mona Hatoum. More noticeable have been the artist-run initiatives and off-site interventions in houses themselves in Europe and Britain such as the infamous "Chambres d'Amis" in Ghent (1986),"Chambre 763" in Paris (1994) and Martin Vincent's "Annual Programme" of house-bound exhibitions which have caught the spirit of domestic resurgence.[12]

It is the displacement of the domestic to the gallery environment and its use to communicate ideas beyond the subversion of domesticity that has produced the context and impetus for this exhibition. Claustrophobia emerged from the legacy of this axial network of projects and exhibitions, but consciously as an embrace of diverse practices, as opposed to a homogenising framework. The exhibition has developed as a series of interconnecting journeys through interiors, windows, doorways and screens; views out and in, through, above and under: always marked by the absence of any human presence.

The works act as the architecture of our myths, politics and memories, but are also clearly the prosthetics for our selves. Rachel Whiteread's "Torso", a cast of the inside of a hot water-bottle, acts within the exhibition as an inversion of the

10 See Rozsika Parker, "Housework", Spare Rib, 1975, no.26, p.38
11 Haar and Reed, op. cit.
12 See Michael Wilson, "Gallery at Home: Part 1", Artists Newsletter, November 1997, p. 10-12, "Gallery at Home: Part 2", December 1997, p. 10-12 and "Gallery at Home: Part 3", Artists Newsletter, February 1998, p. 10-12

associations of the domestic object (in this case warmth and comfort), but also mimics a truncated sarcophagus. Everyday objects mimic the human form and thus once redundant, remade or transformed lead us back to ourselves. As Jean-Paul Sartre once commented, "the bomb which destroys my house also destroys my body insofar as my house was already an indication of my body."[13]

What immediately becomes apparent in the assemblance of these works in the gallery is their apparent inappropriateness for the public realm. Displaced into this clinical environment for public examination, their affiliation to a private world is heightened. We respond to the intimacy of bed, carpet and wallpaper, to the seductiveness of the familiar. Each of the works plays upon this device of seduction and subsequent disruption to produce a series of reactions, which could be characterised as "uncanny". The genre of the uncanny, explored with particular relevance to this exhibition in Anthony Vidler's "The Architectural Uncanny"[14], was originally described by Freud as that "class of the frightening which leads back to what is known of old and long familiar".[15] As Jon Bird noted in relation to Rachel Whiteread's monumental public sculpture, "House",

"Side-on, the squat geometry of "House", with its vertical and horizontal divisions and interior details, offered a reassuring familiarity - we know this vocabulary and can imaginatively recreate the routines of daily life. But there was a difference. This might be recognised as a disturbance located between perception and cognition; as the uncanniness of the object

13 Jean-Paul Sartre, Being and Nothingness, New York, 1956, p. 325
14 Anthony Vidler, The Architectural Uncanny: Essays in the Modern Unhomely, MIT Press, 1992
15 Sigmund Freud, "The Uncanny", Standard Edition of the Complete Psychological Works, vol. XVII, trans. James Strachey, et. al, The Hogarth Press and The Institute of Psycho-Analysis, 1953

invaded the symbolic field leaving the viewer estranged from everyday normality - the everyday itself becomes strange."[16] In this manner, the artists here disrupt the comfort of nostalgia. James Casebere's fork punctures the retro-chic of the fifties fridge, whilst Howard Arkley's chromatic patterning jars the exoticism of the Australian suburban interior. Both photograph and painting are constructed through constituent parts which resist the theatrical suspension of disbelief inherent in the illusionistic representation of domestic space. So too, the implied tension between violence and fragility in the work of Doris Salcedo and Nina Saunders short-circuits the de-politicisation of these highly poetic works. In literally confronting the spectator with their own image and set of memories, values and interpretations, Mat Collishaw's "Enchanted Wardrobe" embodies the underlying pattern of uncanny encounters, a maze of enchantment and disenchantment.

The displaced sculptural objects of Salcedo and Rachel Whiteread and the photographs of Melanie Friend and Carrie Mae Weems, commemorate unspecified occurrences. "Whose memory is it that we experience, for whom and how do we remember?" Charles Merewhether has asked of Salcedo's work. "Is the memory of the fallen, the subject of violence or oppression, remembered forever too late? Can it be more than a gesture of redemption for the living?"[17]

The soundtrack of Albanian voices testifying to the violent acts of Serbian police which contexualises Melanie Friend's 1995 photographs of Kosovan homes and the rhythmic ballads of West African beliefs which attend Weems' photographs of the Gullah Island huts, reassert the unspoken. They give the absent residents the power of voice. The silence of nostalgia is shattered. Salcedo's process of investigation in Bogotá is intimate and cumulative. The stories told to her emerge not through the mouthpiece of reportage or photo-journalism, but through the metaphor of remnants of an existence with which diverse audiences might identify. The clothes and objects are

16 Jon Bird, "dolce domum", House, Phaidon Press Limited, 1995, p. 119
17 Charles Merewether, "To Bear Witness", Doris Salcedo, New Museum of Contemporary Art, New York & Site Santa Fe, 1998, p. 21

caught within the cement-filled cabinet as if frozen by a
Vesuvian eruption, at a moment of extreme violence.

If these objects and images operate in some ways as
memorials or monuments through the collective consciousness
of the shared meanings of the domestic, they do so by refusing
the permanence and anonymity of the public monument. Here
the legacy of "Womanhouse" and "Housework", "the personal
as political", creeps into the artists' processes. The seeming
frivolity of Kathy Temin's 1969 bubble TV, perched on the
picnic box and framed by the rumpus room felt wall, is
transformed by the scrolling letter on screen. Written by
her father, it relates his search for other Temins who might
have survived the Holocaust. As an indoor monument, the
work aptly combines the complex forms of portraiture,
commemoration and documentation. So too Meyer Vaisman's
previous series of installations entitled "Green on the Outside,
Red on the Inside", culminate here in an impenetrable
entranceway embedded in the wall of the gallery. Using the
impermanent structures of the pre-fab, the entry and view into
Vaisman's own private space is now blocked, where previously
one could peer into reconstructions of his childhood home.

The structures here suggest their own specific histories -
pre-fabricated, post-war temporary housing, 1970s suburbia,
and musty Edwardian parlor-life. Middle-class British suburbia
is perhaps most recognisably parodied in Nina Saunders'
new work. As the swing punctures the embossed wallpaper,
Englebert Humperdink's rendition of "Forever" lulls
menacingly, conjuring memories of Alan Ayckbourne's tragedy
of suburban existence "Abigail's Party". The swing is
transformed from an object of play into a weapon of
destruction - or is it survival? "Forever and Ever" - an ode
to everlasting love - becomes a suffocating backing-track to
suburban life.

Charlotte Perkins Gilman's nineteenth-century novella "The
Yellow Wallpaper" employs the wallpapered room to create
a similarly fraught series of associations. Within the story, a
woman is driven slowly mad by her enforced confinement in

a former nursery, hallucinating about the suppressive and consuming nature of the wallpaper itself. The architecture is personified as the repressive force, which must be conquered. Within Carolyn Eskdale's muslin room, the furnishings and structures are doubled, as if mimicking the same psychological disturbance that occurs to Gilman's heroine. This doubling and repetition occurs through the exhibition in the motion of Saunders' swing, in Matthias Müller's filmic narrative, in Casebere's photograph of multiple alcoves; but most noticeably in Eskdale's reformation of gendered space.

If architectural space is constructed socially and culturally, then these associations are most obviously communicated and performed through the stereotype of the housebound TV wife/mother. The "house-wife", that construction of co-dependency between "hoover and her" (so aptly captured in Louise Bourgeois' series of drawings from the late 1940s entitled "Woman-House"), is the missing cardboard cut-out from Arkley's suburban dreams, from Casebere's kitchen sink view, from Mark Bennett's architectural fictions. It is only in Matthias Müller's climatic film montage that female figures appear. Through the repetitive cycles of gestures, all caught within domestic settings, these women are revealed as fictions themselves, however. The artificial, media-generated myths of home life are revealed as mere shadows, which can be fast-forwarded, cut-and-pasted and erased.

As Soo Jin Kim has described in reference to the work of Uta Barth (see below), it would seem that the fiction of domesticity, which frames our experience of private life, can be found almost anywhere and everywhere. Hotel room, foyer, airport lounge - these non-places mimic the place called home. Characteristically unspecific, they are rarely the places remembered. Like Whiteread's casts of non-spaces - under the bed or bath, inside the closet - they are the spaces which witness the everyday rituals or transitions. Barth's photographs are subtle indicators of those moments of recognition, altering our perception of our relation to space.

Permindar Kaur's crate-like room perched tentatively upon

struts as if bound for the fork-lift truck, conceals a non-space itself. The cheap veneer of the walls, standard bedspread and unsympathetic ceiling light mimic the standardisation of a hotel room. And yet, the steel bed is too wide, the walls of the room too close, the ceiling too low and there is an absence of windows. These are the evocations of a nightmare in transit. As in Mona Hatoum's "Doormat", the guise of the familiar yet again betrays a dark and brooding reality. The steel pins which spell out the word "Welcome", like the crashing swing in Saunders' work, create violent barriers to the comforting associations of domesticity.

The knawing absence throughout Claustrophobia is that of the child. Evoked through the objects of play - rumpus room, swing, Batman's cave, beanstalk and hiding places - childhood is that utopian state to which we may never have been, let alone return. Marina Warner has suggested, "You and I, when we long to be as little children can only masquerade as such, we can only perform childlikeness as far as we can observe it or recall it. We are doomed to an ironic innocence."[18] By pausing or transforming the domestic, these artists perform for us the child-like experience of wonder at the everyday.

The experience of these works is certainly one of enchantment. We are no longer in Kansas, the epitome of grey mundanity, but rather encounter lives less ordinary. In a world of enchantment, of fiction, the everyday is transformed - wardrobes lead to magical lands, the miniature becomes the gigantic, doorways and windows are escape hatches to fantasy; but encounters and rites of passage through fiction and works of art such as these nevertheless lead to an end of innocence. Perhaps Kansas represents for us that place to which we can never return, as Rushdie has suggested, "the place from which we began".

18 Marina Warner, "Little Angels, Little Devils: Keeping Childhood Innocent", Six Myths of Our Time: Managing Monsters: The Reith Lectures, Vintage, 1994, p. 38

Claire Doherty
Curator

"In contrast to the ambivalent - even antagonistic - relationship between domesticity and modernism, the post-modern era has witnessed a kind of homecoming in high culture, as artists and designers have (re)turned their attention to domesticity... Specifically, the idea of home today is caught between the stasis of nostalgia, historical fantasy and dynamism of activist engagement with the future; on one hand, the home functions as a potent image or symbol, on the other it exists in all the complexity of daily experience in a three-dimensional world."

Sharon Haar and Christopher Reed, "Coming Home: A Postscript on Postmodernism", *Not at Home: The Suppression of Domesticity in Modern Art and Architecture*, Thames and Hudson, 1996, p. 253

Howard Arkley

Home Beautiful

"Arkley's homes are far from ironic - they appear as if painted by a proud owner. Yet, ironically, given Arkley's engagement with feminism, it was the suburbs that feminists often accused of locking women into the subordinate role of home-maker. The movement which had motivated his earlier work could be seen in his celebration of the house, regarded throughout the modern era as a woman's domain, far from the masculine world of work...the Australian raison d'être is to own one's own home, and here that ambition was writ large and loud as Arkley took the house as commodity and rendered its marketable façade with a Pop aesthetic. This was a Pop sensibility attuned to the Antipodes and pulsing with knowing and self-awareness...

Like Pop artists, Arkley's appropriations are elegies to a consumer culture, one that could include images of art histories like de Stijl alongside hardware catalogues of do-it-yourself decoration. Here the museum without walls met wallpaper.

A Romantic notion of creativity infuses all of Arkley's work. During this period and despite the apparent banality of his sub-ject matter, Arkley was passionate about his choice of imagery and his approach to his work...Arkley leapt into the interior of his suburban homes like a maverick prodigal son. Yet despite his passion for suburbia, there is a constant sense of distance in Arkley's work: the distance of time evident in the nostalgia of his patterning; the distance from the canvas achieved by using the airbrush; the distance from realism in his Modernist

Deluxe Setting 1992
acrylic on canvas
173 x 135 cm

Collection Brian & Kalli Rolfe,
Melbourne. Photo: Courtesy Tolarno
Galleries, Melbourne

Interior Tableau 1992
acrylic on canvas 173 x 135cm
Private Collection Melbourne.
Photo: Courtesy Tolarno Galleries, Melbourne

subversion of colour and perspective; the emotional distancing inherent in his unpeopled suburban environments; the distance from the personal implied by what appear to be standardised house plans.

His homes are formulaic, prefabricated structures, stressing the notion that the average homebuyer has neither the time nor the money for indulging the fantasies of architects. Similarly, with his mass-market wallpaper patterns, it is as if Arkley as decorator is so enamoured with each and every pattern on offer that he cannot decide which one to use. Yet this apparently undisciplined desire to utilise everything at hand in fact relies on considerable technical skill and control in order to combine the patterns into an overall whole - measuring one pattern off against another to narrowly avoid a sense of pattern overload.

Thus the formal aspects of these works are crucial. Not only do they hold the compositions together, they also conspire against any simple reading of the works as mere narratives or studies in loneliness. Arkley is not trying to draw the viewer's attention to the lack of people but to the tricks of the light he performs, the painterly balancing act he pulls off. There is a glowing sense of pride in the loving decoration of each room and façade, which suggests the presence of those who live there. A gas heater burns brightly and chairs are arranged for their occupants - but the owners are outside the picture frame, where we, the viewers, stand, presumably happily admiring their hearth. These houses and interiors are our own."

Extracts from Ashley Crawford and Ray Edgar, *Spray:
The Work of Howard Arkley*, A World Art Book, Craftsman House, 1998,
p. 88-89 and 111

Uta Barth

The Space of Non-Place

The captain announces that we're flying over Seoul now, ready to make the final descent. I look out of the window, at the grey-green grid below, at the city my neighbours and I will descend and disperse into. It looks just like Los Angeles when we took off.

At the airport, I walk through hallways lined with welcoming posters, travelling quickly from a beach in Tahiti, to a penthouse in New York, a ski lounge in Switzerland, from poster to poster. Suitcases and boxes come tumbling down the chute, and slowly circle around and around adding to the nausea from the turbulent flight. I accidentally grab a piece of luggage that looks like mine but with someone else's tag, arguing with its rightful owner as my own case circles past me amidst the confusion.

The city through the window of the cab looks unfamiliar and I'm thankful that the radio is playing a song I know. Immense flower arrangements, sparkling chandeliers, an overabundance of chairs, and people in long lines crowd the hotel lobby. In my small room are two beds, a lamp, bathroom, a telephone, lock on the door, and a window to look out of. The bed still feels warm with a faint trace of the previous guest. I hear a few muffled voices over the sound of traffic, but they're never loud enough to decipher what language they're speaking in. The air is made artificially cold so that I am aware of the warmth of my own body, without actually being cold myself. I look across this city I don't know and I feel at home.

Highways, airports, train stations, supermarkets, and hotel rooms make up a new landscape of spaces that are 'out-of-place' with the rest of the surroundings. Anonymous and self-sufficient, these and similar 'non-places' appear across different countries bringing with them an uncanny sense of familiarity while hardly showing a trace of local specificity or exoticism. They can exist in any country yet remain ultimately interchangeable. In these non-places, the subject experiences an emptying of individuality, in which only the movement of fleeting images enables the observer to hypothesise the existence of a past and glimpse

right
Ground #52, 1995
colour photograph
9.75" x 12"
Photo: Paula Goldman
Courtesy London Projects,
London

left
Ground #35, 1994,
colour photograph,
19.5" x 20.5"
Photo: Paula Goldman
Courtesy London Projects,
London

the possibility of a future. Everything proceeds as if space had been trapped by time, as if there were no history other than the most recent memory.

Space emerges from this lack of context charged with potential. Free of specificity, non-places arrange and rearrange their co-ordinates in an infinite number of ways, becoming amorphous as well as ubiquitous, space becomes uprooted, unlocated, and interchangeable. Once it gains the potential to be more than one place, it has a freedom akin to the boundlessness of the imagination.

As the ease and speed of international travel shrinks the world, the terminals for the traveller (hotels, stations, airports, etc.) become extensions of the no-place of travel, the dislocation of being on the move. The subject dissolves into them. Identity surrenders to anonymity, enabling the passive joys of facelessness or the more active pleasures of imagining. As a result of the banality or familiarity of non-places, everything in sight falls secondary to the stillness and solitude of the space. The act of looking encompasses the

Ground #66, 1996
colour photograph
19.5" x 20.5"
Courtesy London Projects, London

subject, and takes precedence over the object of the gaze. The eye, attempting to make distinctions, sees sameness instead of difference; as the subject, hypnotised by nothingness, becomes blind to the world of non-place. The world dematerialises as the focus shifts from manifestation to perception: a thunderstorm passing, changing the landscape is made less momentous in comparison to the remoteness of the space the viewer inhabits, the profound slowness of time passing, and the immense emptiness of the room.

Non-places, developing with the modern affects of detachment, extreme speed, and interminable waiting, point to a world thus surrendered to solitary privatisation. Though these spaces evoke a sense of lonely individuality, it is precisely individuality that is being dissolved, that is lost. Like being in Kansas and Oz at the same time, the subject splits and loses the sense of individuality to individuation in non-places, what Margaret Morse refers to as being motionless at the vortex of speed. Here, a new kind of seeing subject exists, a kind of mutant: one who sees itself looking from the vantagepoint of being nowhere and elsewhere simultaneously. What the viewer confronts in every non-place is an image of self: the only face to be seen, the only voice to be heard, is one's own, yet echoed by millions of others in other non-places.

Once home, my things sit just as I left them. I hear my neighbours through the thin walls; the bass of a boom-box reverberates nearby. I open some windows for air, and look out the window. I see the same landscape I've seen before, in other countries that share little in common with the culture here. The world seems closer.

Soo Jin Kim

Soo Jin Kim is an artist, writer and filmmaker who lives and works in Los Angeles. Her work and films have been exhibited internationally and she has published in Art and Design, (UK); Framework, (USA) and Parallax (UK) and has edited an anthology of criticism, fiction, and poetry entitled Things That Quicken The Heart. Currently, she teaches at Otis College of Art and Design, Art Center College of Design, and Loyola Marymount University in Los Angeles.

Untitled (98.5), 1998
edition of 5
triptych of colour photographs
38" x 197.5"
Courtesy London Projects, London

Mark Bennett

Imaginary Spaces:
The Architecture of the Television Family

"Television set design is no accident. The television narrative, like that of classical Hollywood cinema, uses set design to create a sense of space that attracts the viewer's attention, affording us the illusion of being present at the scene of the action. In a very real sense, the ability of any television show to effectively tell a story is dependent upon the production techniques used in its creation. Think for a moment of how the design of M*A*S*H, with its sets of great intricacy and depth of field, lent itself so well to the complex interaction of multiple characters, whereas the shallow space of the Brady household reinforced the constricted world of this singular family...

Our utter familiarity with these pieces of imaginary architecture coincided with the emergence of television as a cultural force in the 1950s. Perhaps the most startling aspect of post-war economy - and one which certainly had the greatest impact on television - was the astounding expansion of the middle class...

By the end of the 1950s, the penetration of the television set into American homes had reached near-saturation levels. Yet even as television established itself as an indispensable domestic appliance, television programs began to reflect the suburban milieu, carefully retaining the more theatrical presentation codes of narrative realism. This shift reflected the medium's commercialism. Television in this sense helped usher in an age which saw the rise of the privatised home

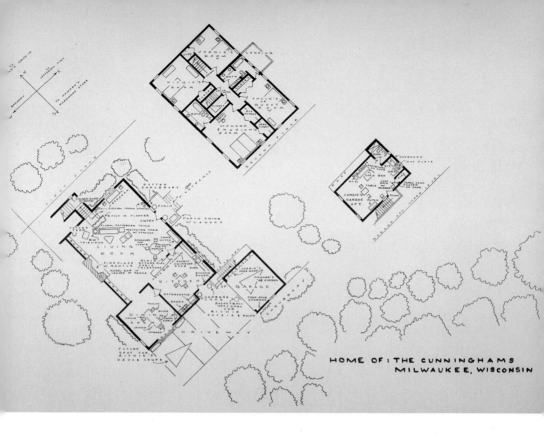

HOME OF: THE CUNNINGHAMS
MILWAUKEE, WISCONSIN

Home of the Cunninghams 1995
ink and pencil on graph vellum paper, 24" x 36" sheet
Collection Eric Mellencamp, Seal Beach, California

replete with "durable goods" and "home appliances", everything from toasters to automobiles to radio and television sets. After all, these commodities of middle-class affluence were omnipresent in television advertising. This signification extends well beyond the commercials themselves and into actual programming. The variety of genres - domestic melodrama, game show, and situation comedy - not only entertain us, they define and reinforce the values we as Americans place on various commodities related to an urban or suburban lifestyle. In this sense, the broadcast institutions themselves exist as massive, on-going advertising agencies for the American Way of Life, celebrating a commonality of vision that encompasses the lifestyles and values that characterise our cultural community...

Whether portraying the rather flat urban design of Ricky

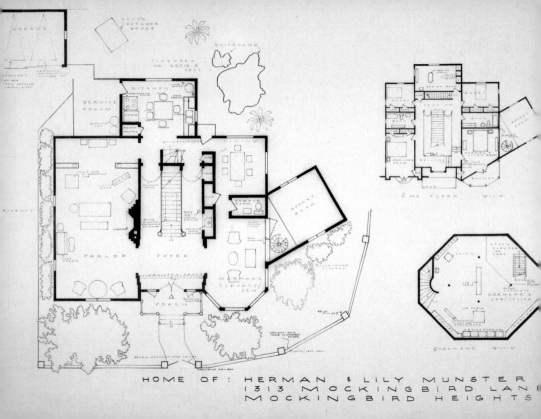

HOME OF: HERMAN & LILY MUNSTER
1313 MOCKINGBIRD LANE
MOCKINGBIRD HEIGHTS

and Lucy Ricardo's Manhattan apartment or a more complex domestic space like that of Ward and June Cleaver, television has always tried to give the viewer what media scholar Lynn Spigel calls the "perfect view".[1] In other words, the set design attempts to provide a world view that encapsulates both the actions and the intimate lives of characters. Without this dual function, we wouldn't have Mark Bennett's work. The value and delight of his architectural renderings doesn't derive from his rearticulation of these shows as works of art, but rather from the simple fact that he has made manifest what the rest of us only vaguely recognise; without ever actually walking into these places, we know these spaces like we know our own homes. Bennett's drawings confirm the supremacy of television as our primary cultural storyteller. Bill Moyers once described television, in an explicit acknowledgement of the medium's bardic function, as the "campfire around which our nation-tribe sits to weave and re-weave its traditions and tales."[2] As products of the suburban television age, Bennett's work speaks to us in a way that other art simply cannot. We are defined by television; it is our art form, the true expression of late twentieth-century America. Within the walls of the imaginary spaces, Bennett illustrates, all of our culture's ideas and assumptions are contested. For better and worse, this is where we live."

Notes
1. Lynn Spigel, "Installing the Television Set: Popular Discourses on Television and Domestic Space, 1948-55", Camera Obscura 16, January 1988, pp. 11-48
2. Bill Moyers, Channels, October - November 1981, p. 23

Extracts from Mike Mashon, "Imaginary Spaces: The Architecture of the Television Family", in Mark Bennett: TV Sets and the Suburban Dream, The Corcoran Gallery of Art, Washington, 1997. Mike Mashon is Curator at the Motion Picture, Broadcasting and Recorded Sound Division at the Library of Congress, Washington D.C.

James Casebere

Interview between
James Casebere and Jeff Rian

"James Casebere: When I started building models to photograph twenty years ago, I was looking for a combination of humour and horror, a synthesis of the mundane and not so mundane, and a connection between social and personal history. I liked the way Faulkner told a family history in relation to larger social and historical perspectives and a sense of place. I was reading Gaston Bachelard and was also interested in the way conceptual artists like Vito Acconci, Dan Graham, Robert Morris, Alice Aycock and Siah Armajani were moving into sculpture with an architectural orientation. Photography tied into history, myth, and social identity - history being something reconstructed time and again, and twisted to meet the needs of those writing it. Many of my earlier images were about American identity and archetypes. Now they're more generic, and my sources go back further in time and through different cultures...

Jeff Rian: You isolate the traits of a particular kind of place and then build a set piece, without the details that are required in, say, novel writing. Are these skeletal mise-en-scénes for an implied morality play? Or the bare bones of human socialisation told through modes of containment?

JC: In part, it's about the creation of my own subjectivity through a process of construction. It's also a metaphor for the way individuality is defined by culture.

JR: How did you get from courtrooms and westerns to pensive, claustrophobic interiors?

JC: There is a logic to my work - a conscious purpose - which began with images of home, and all the Bachelard-like associations. These were based on my immediate environment and memories of places I'd known. Then I began to think a little about the sociology and history of the perverted ideal that I grew up in the mid-western suburb. This led me to the Arts and Crafts movement and the Bungalow Craze. I went further back, historically, to Shingle Style in New England in the 1870s, which led me to what was happening in the American West at the same time. I made a number of photos about the myth of the American West, first as created in pulp fiction and then as it developed in early cinema. Here was an art form imbued with mythical themes based on popular exchange and the desires of its audience. It was Pop art. Americans had the same needs and impulses when they elected a cowboy president in Ronald Regan, as if public policy had been dictated by psychic needs and projections. I saw this as destructive...

A few years ago my work was inspired by prison history and the Quaker prison reform movement of the early nineteenth century and all its monastic associations. Since then I have been working with larger public corridors and circulation spaces...

In the back of my mind were seventeenth-century northern European paintings of men dwarfed in enormous church vaults. I built two other models. The first was called *Nine Alcoves,* 1995, based on a short novel by Samuel Beckett called The Lost Ones, which takes place in a single circular room packed with people and no apparent way out. Occupants wait in line to climb up into an alcove for a moment of solitude or separation...

While on the one hand I'm now looking at older and more generic architecture, the spaces I'm exploring are partly a reflection of my studio; about the time and labour it takes to make the sets and to take the picture. Isolation versus the pleasure of solitude. It's some kind of dialogue between control and surrender; between the need to have every grain of sand on the floor in exactly the right place, versus leaving it alone. To just stop messing with it. I think this is what I want to evoke. In a way I'm back to the fork in the refrigerator. The room is really the same, only now there is no character, no anthropomorphic figure. The viewer is the character in the room - hopefully feeling the same dread, isolated tension, and sometimes freedom, boredom, and surprise; which is what the process is all about."

Extracts from *Interview between James Casebere and Jeff Rian,*
published in *Flash Art* #200, May - June, 1997. Jeff Rian is a writer based in Paris.

Golden Apple 1986,
silver gelatin print, 30" x 40"
Courtesy Sean Kelly Gallery, New York

Mat Collishaw

Drawers, chests and wardrobes

"Wardrobes with their shelves, desks with their drawers, and chests with their false bottoms are veritable organs of the secret psychological life. Indeed, without these, "objects" and a few others in equally high favour, our intimate life would lack a model of intimacy. They are hybrid objects, subject objects. Like us, through us and for us, they have a quality of intimacy.

Does there exist a single dreamer of words who does not respond to the word wardrobe?...

And to fine words correspond fine things, to grave-sounding words, an entity of depth. Every poet of furniture - even if he be a poet in a garret, and therefore has no furniture - knows that the inner space of an old wardrobe is deep. A wardrobe's inner space is also intimate space, space that is not open to just anybody...

In the wardrobe there exists a centre of order that protects the entire house against uncurbed disorder. Here order reigns, or rather, this is the reign of order. Order is not merely geometrical; it can also remember the family history...

But the real wardrobe is not an everyday piece of furniture. It is not opened everyday, and so, like a heart that confides in no-one, the key is not on the door.

-L'armoire était sans clefs!...Sans clefs la grande armoire
On regardait souvent sa porte brune et noire
Sans clefs!...C'était étrange! - On rêvait bien des fois
Aux mystères dormant entre ses flancs de bois
Et l'on croyait ouir, au fond de la serrure
Béante, un bruit lointain, vague et joyeux murmure.[1]

(The wardrobe had no keys!...No keys had the big wardrobe
Often we used to look at its brown and black door
No keys!...It was strange! Many a time we dreamed
Of the mysteries lying dormant between its wooden flanks
And we thought we heard, deep in the gaping lock
A distant sound, a vague and joyful murmur.)

Enchanted Wardrobe, 1994
wooden wardrobe, 2 way mirror, sensor, florescent tubes,
225 x 130 x 70 cm
Collezione Re Rebaudengo Sandretto, Torino.
Photo: Courtesy Lisson Gallery, London.

Here Rimbaud designates a perspective of hope: what good things are being kept in reserve in the locked wardrobe? This time it is filled with promise, it is something more than a family chronicle.

André Breton, with a single word, shows us the marvels of unreality by adding a blessed impossibility to the riddle of the wardrobe. In *Revolver aux cheveux blancs* he writes with typical surrealist imperturbability:

L'armoire est pleine de linge
Il y a même des rayons de lune que je peux déplier.

(The wardrobe is filled with linen
There are even moonbeams which I can unfold.)

This carries the image to a point of exaggeration that no reasonable mind would care to attain. But exaggeration is always at the summit of any living image. And to add fantasy linen is to draw a picture, by means of a volute of words, of all the superabundant blessings that lie folded in piles between the flanks of an abandoned wardrobe...If we give objects the friendship they should have, we do not open a wardrobe without a slight start. Beneath its russet wood, a wardrobe is a very white almond. To open it, is to experience an event of whiteness."

Notes
1 Arthur Rimbaud, *Les ètrennes des orphelins*
2 Gaston Bachelard, *The Poetics of Space*, trans. Maria Jolas, Beacon Press, 1969, p. 4

Extracts from Gaston Bachelard, *The Poetics of Space*, trans. Maria Jolas, translation ©1958 Presses Universitaires de France. Translation © 1964 The Orion Press, Inc. Used by permission of Viking Penguin, a division of Penguin Putnam Inc.

Caroline Eskdale

Furnishings

I

My grandmother never remarried after her husband died. As a child, I used to stay at her place every Friday night. It was a large house full of empty rooms. As I lay in bed, from down the hall, from behind my half-closed bedroom door and the half-closed door of her sitting room, the muffled voices of the TV, or TV laughter, carried. Sometimes she would laugh too, once or twice, the sound so fleshed-out, so immediate, compared to the remoteness of the soundtracks.

My grandmother's bedroom, through the middle door off the hall: on the right are two single beds a few feet apart, Edwardian bedheads with curved bedposts to the wall, two sash windows at the end of the room, a French-polished dressing table positioned in between with its large mirror tilted slightly forward.

The bedspreads are white sateen and have skirts which just touch the floor, gathered in folds from the piping at the beds' edges. The fabric across the flats of both beds is completely smooth, with a slight gloss to it. An extra length of the bedspread is designed to fold back over the pillow - in this case, two freshly plumped up, down-filled pillows to each bed.

There is a lamp on a small bedside table. Next to the lamp is a hardback library book covered in protective matt plastic, the fringed end of a suede bookmark protrudes from between the pages. It is the room of a married couple, one of whom

died ten years previously in the bed farthest from the windows, of cancer.

In the kitchen, the floor is highly polished linoleum, deep red; tiny circular indentations mark its surface: they're imprints left by metal studs used to reinforce women's high-heel shoes from the fifties. They create tracks between the backdoor and two other doors which lead off the kitchen, they cluster around the stove from the days of large dinner parties.

My grandmother used to polish the mahogany dining table with a soft mustard-coloured cloth, its edges stitched with rust-coloured thread. She would enfold her hand in this cloth and pass the flat of her palm around and around against the gleaming wood, run it down carved legs which bulged at the middle, tapered towards the floor, their feet resting on thick chunks of blue glass designed to support a billiard table. She would only pass her cloth-wrapped hand once or twice up and down each leg, almost as if she wasn't doing it at all.

II

As a boy, my father was interned in a Japanese Prisoner of War camp in Sumatra. When the Japanese soldiers first arrived, in 1942, they began rounding up most Europeans, knocking on doors, sending families out onto the streets. Local Indonesians ran into the just-deserted houses in order either to "loot", or reclaim some colonial wealth. He described furniture belonging in the family home being carried out: wardrobes with their doors swinging open, clothes spilling; men with chairs strapped to their backs; a boy running with hands full of piano keys, carried like bouquets; women with cutlery, wine glasses clustered at the stems, gathered so tight they split open against each other.

III

I think of the furniture that Carolyn Eskdale utilises in her work as being Edwardian. It may not be, but that's the impression it leaves. A kind of melancholy. An austerity. Quiet ordered rooms. A sitting-room in which the light is permanently dim, front windows shaded by the veranda outside. Seen through the screen of memory. White lace

Reflected furniture image, 1998
Computer manipulated photo

curtains, or nylon, gathered aside and clasped in a loop of the same fabric, like a small belt.

The cushion on one of the armchairs has an almost imperceptible concavity where the stuffing has been compacted. It is positioned next to the window and has a clear view of the front gate. All down the street are similarly formatted houses, with rooms for sitting and waiting in. This is a country town in central Victoria, established during the gold-rush late last century. Beneath roads and foundations of houses are seams of quartz, strata of clay, hollows of disused mine shafts. Sometimes at night there's the scent of earth from far beneath the surface, an exuded dampness.

Saskia Beudel

Saskia Beudel is a Melbourne based writer who has published short fiction and art reviews. She is currently writing her first novel and is a Masters candidate in the English/Cultural Studies Department, University of Melbourne. She is also the 1998 recipient of the Felix Meyer Travelling Scholarship.

Melanie Friend

Homes and Gardens
Documenting the Invisible: Images of Kosovo

"My husband was in Austria visiting our son, when the police
came here. There were about seventy, kicking the doors,
chasing around my mentally handicapped son. They asked,
"Where is your husband?" My husband has a permit for a gun;
I brought the gun and one policeman hit me hard in the face. I
fell to the ground and was unconscious for three hours. Later
I was told that everyone was screaming, my two boys were
beaten in the yards and were left with bleeding hands. When
my family said they must send me to hospital, the police said,
"It's nothing if an Albanian dies." Now I have hypertension
and high blood pressure and at night, I have nightmares of
my sons being beaten. The police thought they'd killed me
so they didn't stay more than an hour."

October, 1995

*Homes and Gardens: documenting
the invisible: images of Kosovo, 1995*

"The most widely experienced form of police violence in Kosovo province is that undergone by families during police searches for arms. These have become a prominent feature of policing in Kosovo since the outbreak of armed conflict in former Yugoslavia in 1991. Over the past year arms searches have increased dramatically, and are now conducted on a daily basis, most intensively in border villages and rural areas...Because of the traditional pattern of settlement in rural areas of Kosovo, in which large extended families tend to live together, police raids are normally witnessed and personally experienced by many relatives...Accounts of arms searches repeatedly refer to the deliberately intimidating and destructive way in which they are conducted: furniture is broken up, the inmates of the house are threatened, shouted and sworn at, and the men of the house are frequently arrested and beaten in local police stations or, even more humiliatingly, in their homes in front of their families...While most police violence is directed against adult males, in some instances the elderly, women or children who are members of the family have not been spared beatings. Some families have been repeatedly searched by police officers who have shouted at them "Get out of here" or "Go to Albania"."

Extracts from "Yugoslavia: Police violence in Kosovo province - the victims",
Amnesty International Report, September 1994, pp. 7-8

"Clashes have been fiercest in Donje Prekaze village where Serbian forces reportedly used mortars to shell the village houses. They claimed that ethnic Albanians were armed with machine guns and hand-held rocket launchers. The focus of these operations seemed to be houses belonging to the extended family of Adem Shaban Jashari, aged 43, an ethnic Albanian. Belgrade television broadcast images of buildings that appeared to have been shelled, claiming they were the Jashari family compound; bodies were also reportedly visible strewn on the ground. News programs have also broadcast images of an armoured personnel carrier or tank demolishing a building believed to be one of the Jashari houses."

Extract from "Federal Republic of Yugoslavia - ethnic Albanians in Kosovo province",
Amnesty International, Urgent Action Report, 10 March 1998

"Sometimes I think I would rather die than live in this fear."

October, 1995

Doormat 1996
stainless steel pins,
nickel-plated pins, glue, canvas
3 x 71 x 40.5cm
Collection of the artist

Mona Hatoum

"Mona Hatoum is always travelling. The existence of the contemporary artist with any sort of international profile is, in any case, a peripatetic one, but Hatoum admits that there is another kind of necessity to her frequent trips away from home. At its root is, amongst other things, the question of exactly where home is. Trained and based in London, she found herself forced to stay here in the mid-70s when the outbreak of war in the Lebanon prevented her return home to Beirut after a holiday. Her parents, had in their turn, settled there after having had to leave Haifa on the establishment of the state of Israel. Location - not only where one is and how one relates to one's surroundings, but also how one establishes difference from others in being who one is - is a central issue in Hatoum's work. The uncertainty as to cultural place manifests itself in a number of ways. Forms turn themselves inside out or upside down. Likewise, the body refuses to be bounded by its skin and reveals instead its inner workings to the audience's gaze. Artist and viewer change roles. Scale shifts unnervingly. The effect of all these factors is that there is no space that is proper to things, that unequivocally belongs to them. Instead, a site is occupied provisionally and, in many cases, precariously. Seats, beds, floor coverings and even sometimes the floors themselves are treacherous. One does not know where one stands...

Incommunicado, 1993, a metal infant's cot of the sort used in hospitals, has its mattress base made not from substantial metal springs, but from lengths of murderously thin, cheese-cutter wire. One of the first mat pieces, *Prayer Mat*, 1995, has a compass fitted into it so that it can indeed be turned with confidence towards Mecca. The nap of the mat, though, has been created by pushing pins through every hole in the weave of the backing canvas, rendering it impossible to use as a kneeling surface without causing considerable physical damage...

One formal resource that has remained consistent in Hatoum's work is that of minimalism. The simple rectangles of the various mat pieces laid on the floor, the basic shapes of *Socle du Monde* or *Divan Bed*, 1996, the teasing of visual richness from the simplest of materials as in *Light Sentence* and a frequently used chromatic spareness all signal an interest in the eloquence of form. It is an interest which insists that the possibility of meaning arises in an encounter with the work itself rather than that the work act as a conduit for some overlaid narrative or message...The imposition of place by external agencies of which these sculptures speak is striking, the more so because of the domestic cast of the materials Hatoum has used. Household items - a colander, a grater, a milk-strainer - continued to be examined in the Shaker settlement (during Hatoum's residency)...the work produced bears witness to a belief in the essential fluidity of existence. Movement, contact, experience, exchange, memory and many other factors enable us to construct a provisional base from which to operate from moment to moment, but the inadequacy of such a base in the face of the future is inevitable. There is a freedom in understanding this, but as Hatoum's art reveals, it is not without its terrors."

Extracts from Michael Archer, "Mona Hatoum", in *Echolot*, Museum Fridericianum, Kassel, 1998, pp. 25-7

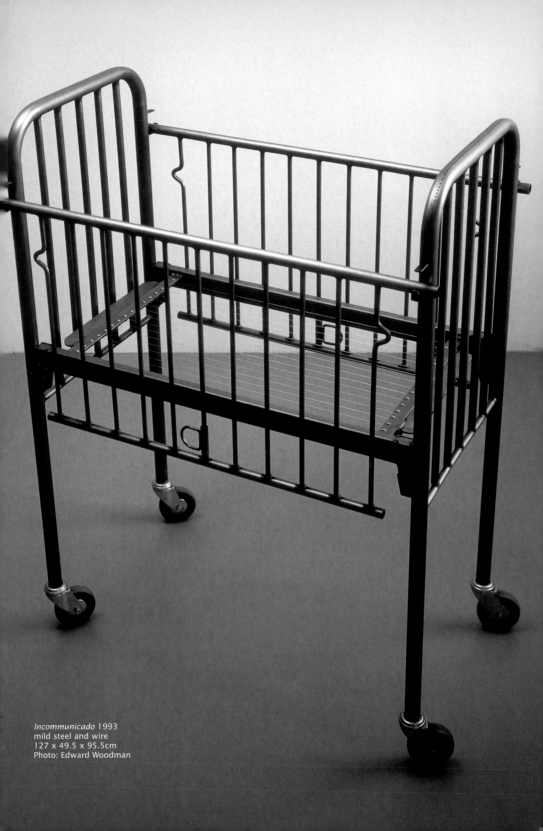

Incommunicado 1993
mild steel and wire
127 x 49.5 x 95.5cm
Photo: Edward Woodman

The Silent Partner 1998
steel bed, wooden box, light
approx 250 x 250 cm

Permindar Kaur

The Silent Partner

You cannot enter this exhibit without commitment. You may open the door and view but you cannot experience without entry. The dynamics of the space come into play immediately and visually from the open door, but the interaction of the visitor with the space properly occurs when the individual both bodily and spiritually, yields to the interior. To appreciate this space, you must enter it alone and submit yourself to whatever feelings surface. One has to yield control and one has to trust. Swift escape from danger is not possible and by placing ourselves in such a position we oppose our most primitive instinct.

The need for an available escape route forms part of the evolutionary theory of Appleton (1975) who emphasised the importance of places which offered both prospect and refuge to our forebears. The ability to spot prey far off and to escape from predators contributed to survival. Such places remain favoured in our own generation. This space fails to support either. It is not possible to see out and it is not possible to escape. By entering the cube, we are forced to face those inner thoughts, fears and memories which will inevitably surface in this environment of no distractions.

Because the interior symbolises both security and confinement, it presents us with the human dilemma, the urge to return to the security of the womb balanced against the need for freedom to expand and explore. Other stresses between security and threat are implicit in the space. The primal image of refuge proposed by Bachelard; the need for

The Silent Partner 1998
steel bed, wooden box, light
approx 250 x 250cm

withdrawal into the shell (1964, p.16) is challenged in this
space by an aversion to being buried alive in the same shell.
Similar archetypal images of the home, originally proposed by
Jung as refuge and hearth (1969) battle those of procreation,
birth and death. While many of the tensions exist at the
unconscious level, there are others which are more superficial.

On the more conscious level, Clare Cooper Marcus (1972)
sees the home as a symbol of the self. As such it is the public
expression of self and represents the identity by which the
individual wishes to be known. Viewed as home, this space
may suggest failure rather than identity, a prison rather than
a refuge.

Research has found that the meaning of any space is
generally different for the layman and the expert. Where the
expert employs an objective and therefore cognitive stance,
the user tends to be more subjective, with the importance
placed on how they are feeling. "Designers tend to react
to environments in perceptual terms (which are their
meanings), whereas the lay public, the users, react to
environments in associational terms." (Rapoport, 1982, p. 19)
Since these associations are learned we can expect to find
individual differences based on differing life experiences and
also differences between cultures as well as the evolutionary
similarities noted previously.

Although the importance of learning is crucial to the human
experience, the ways in which learning occurs may reflect

personally type (Jung, 1923; Keirsey, 1984). Preliminary work by Mithani (1998) finds a correlation between personality type and favourite place. If this is so, then it is equally likely that other aspects of place, such as the importance of familiarity, the amount of space required for comfort, the desire for privacy and the aversion to closed spaces may also reflect personality type.

So, experiencing this enclosure, its immediacy, its connotations, its meaning for any one of us, will reflect our personality and past experiences. Memories and associations will be provoked into consciousness. Both the total enclosure and the bed may provoke a range of responses.

No doubt there will be differing degrees of claustrophobia experienced in this exhibit, but there may also be individuals for whom this space is therapeutic. Entering the space is voluntary and the duration of time spent there on the bed is under the control of the individual. Given the importance of choice, control and privacy to human development it is possible that will be fulfilling. Without such control it would be difficult to see the space as anything other than restrictive and punitive. This may indeed be the intent of the artist, but I suspect that the drama lies more in the examination of the self that is provoked and in the individuality of their conclusion.

Patricia Newell

Notes
J. Appleton, *The Experience of Landscape*, Wiley, London, 1974
G. Bachelard, *The Poetics of Space*, Orion Press, New York, 1964
C.Cooper, *The House as Symbol*, Design and Environment, 14, 178-182, 1972
C. Jung, *Psychological Types*, Harcourt Brace, New York, 1923
D. Keirsey and M. Bates, *Please Understand Me: Character and temperament types*, Gnosology Books, Del Mar, CA, 1984
S. Mithani, *Favourite Places and Personality Type*, unpublished paper, 1998
A. Rapoport, *The Meaning of the Built Environment*, Sage, London, 1982

Patricia Newell is Lecturer in Environmental Psychology in the Department of Psychology at the University of Warwick. She has published papers "A systems model of privacy", *Journal of Environmental Psychology*, 14, 65-78, 1994, "Perspectives on privacy", *Journal of Environmental Psychology*, 15, 87-104, 1995 and "A cross-cultural examination of favourite places", *Environment and Behaviour*, 29, 495-514, 1997.

Matthias Müller

Home Stories

"The 'narrative' of Matthias Müller's *Home Stories* is composed entirely of segmented, repeated actions culled from Hollywood films. These segments centre around repetition, and in so doing, make painfully clear the limited types of activities assigned to female characters in cinematic representations. This tactic illustrates that Hollywood films aren't really remarkably different from 'home movies'. Both reflect the influence of patriarchal standards of representation and representability; and the space of the 'home movie' is informed, even structured, by classical Hollywood images of what a 'home' is.

In other words, 'home,' that space associated with feelings of safety and freedom, becomes somehow alienated from the subject's experience. Life imitates art as 'home' becomes a simulation that eventually takes on nightmarish qualities. The space through which the characters in Müller's film negotiate their everyday activities is now as unreal and estranged from the everyday as would be motion picture representations of it.

As its title suggests, *Home Stories* takes place entirely within the domestic space 'normally' occupied by women in the mainstream texts of the time period from which Müller has chosen his clips. This era, extending roughly from 1950-1965, witnessed the birth of the domestic goddess (in the personae of Donna Reed, Harriet Nelson, and June Cleaver) and the beginnings of domestic commodity fetishism (in the form of pink refrigerators, boomerang tables, butterfly chairs, etc.) The woman was transformed into the 'housewife,' and the home, her world.

After a series of establishing shots drawn from canonical melodramas - shots of interiors of homes identified as ideally bourgeois by their furnishings and décor - Lana Turner (as

Still from Home Stories 1990
(video - duration 6 mins)
Collection of the artist

Still from Home Stories 1990
(video - duration 6 mins)
Collection of the artist

Madame X) is shown lying on a bed covered with a worn chenille bedspread. Her surroundings, although home-like, are decidedly less than comfortable. The cheap furnishings and crumbling interior are rendered even more forbidding by unnatural lighting used to suggest the character's state of mind (she is suffering from absinthe addiction). This shot is followed by a quick montage of other, similarly angst-filled women, all exhibiting physical symptoms of despair. The sequence ends as it began, with Turner as Madame X back in the dingy hotel room. The action has come full circle - we have gone nowhere. The characters remain confined within the closing walls of home, sweet home.

The intercutting of these vignettes illustrates the similarity in spatial representation of 'feminine space' and the restrictive influence this space exerts on the actions of the female characters. These narratives focus exclusively upon differences drawn along gender axes in the construction of their characters. 'Femininity' becomes a constant, a 'given,' that remains firmly located within the domestic space, and that overrides the boundaries of racial, ethnic, geographic, or class distinctions. These women, or more precisely, their representations, become mirror images of one another. Here, Müller lays bare the filmic paranoia latent in these narratives by simply exaggerating (through creative editing of the formerly separate narratives into one) the very codes that define the classical Hollywood melodrama.

Home Stories, in its insistence upon mirroring and self-reflexivity, reveals its source of terror as not something inherently 'feminine', but rather as the construct of femininity created by patriarchal modes of representation and held up as 'mirrors' to women in texts 'designed' for female consumption.

Müller's redesigned text transforms these confined/confining depictions of femininity, and after building to an intertexual frenzy, frees the representations both in terms of the narrative (the final image is of a woman running into the darkness - out of the confines of 'home') and in terms of their cultural usage."

Extract from Robert Cagle, *The Mechanical Reproduction of Melodrama: Home Stories and Gender Critique*, Rochester, NY, 1992. Robert Cagle is a filmmaker and film critic who has written on such subjects as Canadian popular film and the avant-garde. He is currently at work on a book on cult films, tentatively entitled *Cinematic Obsessions*.

Untitled (cement cabinet) 1995
wood, cement, glass, steel, 162 x 99.5 x 37 cm
Caldic Collectie, Rotterdam.
Photo: Courtesy Alexander and Bonin, New York

Doris Salcedo

The Thought from Outside

"This kind of symmetrical conversion is required of the language of fiction. It must no longer be a power that tirelessly produces images and makes them shine, but rather a power that undoes them, that lessens their overload, that infuses them with an inner transparency that illuminates them little by little until they burst and scatter in the lightness of the unimaginable. Blanchot's fictions are, rather than the images themselves, their transformation, displacement, and neutral interstices. They are precise; the only figures they outline are in the grey tones of everyday life and the anonymous. And when wonder overtakes them, it is never in themselves but in the void surrounding them, in the space in which they are set, rootless and without foundation.

The fictitious is never in things or in people, but in the impossible verisimilitude of what lies between them: encounters, the proximity of what is most distant, the absolute dissimulation in our very midst. Therefore, fiction consists not in showing the invisible, but in showing the extent to which the invisibility of the visible is invisible. Thus, it bears a profound relation to space; understood in this way, space is to fiction what the negative is to reflection (whereas dialectical negation is tied to the fable of time). No doubt this is the role that houses, hallways, doors, and rooms play in almost all of Blanchot's narratives: placeless places, beckoning thresholds, closed, forbidden spaces that are nevertheless exposed to the winds, hallways fanned by doors that open rooms for unbearable encounters and create gulfs between them across which voices cannot carry and that even muffle cries: corridors leading to more corridors where the night resounds, beyond sleep, with the smothered voices of those who speak, with the cough of the sick, with the walls of the dying, with the suspended breath of those who ceaselessly cease living; a long and narrow room, like a tunnel, in which approach and distance - the approach of forgetting, the distance of the wait - draw near to one another and unendingly move apart."

Extract from Michel Foucault, "Maurice Blanchot: The Thought from Outside", in *Foucault/Blanchot*, trans. Jeffrey Mehiman and Brian Massumi, New York, Zone Books, 1987, p. xxix, selected by Doris Salcedo.

Untitled (cement chair) 1995
wood, cement, steel: Private Collection.
Photo: Courtesy Alexander and Bonin, New York

Nina Saunders

Forever

When I was six we moved house. To console me for my feelings of uprootedness, my parents let me choose the wallpaper for my new room - a relentlessly repeating pattern of snaking ribbons and pink rosebuds.

If I lay on my back on my bed and squinted my eyes I could make the rosebuds dither and dance. The wallpaper soon got on my nerves. But today, if I half-close my eyes before a pattern of equivalent repetitive insistence, I can still retrieve the minute details, the tastes and smells of my childhood.

Nina Saunders' work pathologises the insistence of such household memories. She collages complexly resonating reminiscences of family and home, holding them strenuously in tension together. Each one of the recalled forms is startlingly specific to a reassuringly suburban taste in post-war England, yet somehow awry. Lovingly revived, painstaking reconstructed, their combined, carefully-judged inconsistencies seem to promise some deeper meaning, forever just beyond our reach.

Her decorative domestic scenarios are labour-intensive, suffocating and, in the perfection of their domestic detail, insistently gendered. They are the spaces of uneasy encounters, and of fraught repetitions. They invite us to interrogate the customary relationships between body and home.

The steady to and fro metronome of Forever's playground swing beats out the passing of time. But it is a time that measures insistently backwards, accompanied by Englebert Humperdink's promise that, whatever lies behind the cracks in

the wallpaper, it will always be with us.

It is not a comfortable thing to confront the past as Nina Saunders excavates it. Vulnerability and risk hover around the peeling back of layers of memory - vulnerability as to what we might find; risk that each layer may simply reveal another, equally familiar yet equally opaque, resisting the recognition which would give us back our childhood innocence.

Nina Saunders has always worked with the detritus of everyday life. The found objects on which she builds bond, home and labour - upholstered step-ladders leading nowhere, discarded chairs, conscientiously reclaimed and filled with household memories. Each completed art-object carries the permanent trace of bruisingly onerous female physical labour - the stitching against resistance required for hand-made upholstery, the layering and overlayering of pattern upon pattern, overwhelming with decorative care.

Her most recent site-specific installations, produced last year for the Bluecoat Gallery in Liverpool, screened the windows of the façade of a children's orphanage - the old Bluecoat Hospital - with buttoned, white-leatherette-upholstered panels (*Pure Thought III*). Inside the austere eighteenth-century building, a gigantic white-upholstered sphere ten foot in diameter (*Pure Thought IV*) almost entirely filled one of the gallery spaces. *Pure Thought IV* was, literally, impossible to grasp - visitors were seen to attempt to encircle it with outstretched arms, which failed to register against its bulk and its unexpectedly ungiving surface. In relation to the memories of this institutional space, the installations denied maternity, held off nurture, reproached the building for its resistance to any memory of childhood.

In *Forever* the excluded child enters the home with the playground swing. But any attempt at innocent play is once again claustrophobically confined, each swing pounding and damaging the enclosing space. And I, at least, if I screw up my eyes, can see my childhood memories dancing on the wallpaper ... or are they, perhaps, struggling to get out from behind its tendrils?

Lisa Jardine

Lisa Jardine is Professor of Renaissance Studies at Queen Mary and Westfield College, University of London, and an author and broadcaster.

Kathy Temin

The Chassis and the Entrails:
The Nature of Recollection

Drawing on materials from her immediate environment and
experience, Kathy Temin has created monuments and
collections.   Her work refers to the suburban home where
she grew up in Australia during the seventies.   The colours,
materials and styles act as a cultural marker of the
psychological and social situation she inhabited.   The rounded,
futuristic, vacuum formed, synthetic aesthetic that she engages
leaves a trail of social and psychological evidence.   This subtext
rests in the shadows of the utopian kitsch look of her physical
objects.   The seventies with its optimism left little room for
the contemplation of the rupture of social space that took
place over that decade.   Temin collects kitsch and places it in
museum-like vitrines reversing its position as the readily
digestible, banal, and trendy stuff of popular culture, turning
it into perplexing and obsessive matter that is inextricably
lodged in our memory.

   If there are two colours that truly embody the seventies
they would be beige and tangerine.   They are both tertiary,
muted, banal, friendly and ubiquitous.   These were the colours
of Kathy Temin's childhood kitchen.   Typical to the middle
class home of the seventies, this is the domain of the maternal:
perfectly pristine, clean Formica continuous countertops, built-
in dishwasher, garbage disposal, and the mix master.   Mission
control for the mother, these domestic headquarters were
where all nurturing and conditioning was disbursed.   Its
pristine state was preserved at all costs.   The garbage disposal

Indoor Monument:
A Monument to the Home
(in the rumpus room video) 1995
installation at Australian Centre for
Contemporary Art, Melbourne.

Some of My Favourite Things 1997
Habitat Store, Tottenham Court Road Store
7.5m x 2.2m x 1.3m and detail

did not breakdown and stink and the mix master never hurt anyone. As long as everything was kept in perfect order there was no danger.

Indoor Monument: A Monument to The Home (in the rumpus room video), 1995 carries on the tradition of the seventies in tranquil beige and tangerine. The monument stands like the robot, R2D2, at rigid attention. His body is a vitrine devoid of any contents, missing its entrails. Resembling the helmet of the space suit worn in *2001: A Space Odyssey*, the TV crowns the top of the monument that is continually printing out its message in bold letters. A high tech letter in a bottle filtered through the futuristic idealism of a seventies' television screen. The letter tells a story of unspeakable loss. The monument's missing interior, the blood and guts, are splattered across its virtual face, betraying its desperate search for its family and home.

Monuments are like shrines, places to remember something that is no longer with us. They mark sanctioned space and express our relationship to that which is no longer present in its natural state. In the same way that we memorialise the past, we also fantasise about the future. Monuments are idealised representations of particular people or events. Coexisting with that ideal image lurks the dark side of what is not represented. It is inevitable that when we separate the thing to be preserved from the cacophony of the lived experience; the pristine monument carries with it the ghost of its own past.

Temin collects objects as an ongoing collage for and of the self and categorises them. In *Some of my Favourite Things*, 1997 Temin brought together parts of her ongoing collection. From magazines with the Australian pop star Kylie Minogue on the cover, to seventies' hairdryers and a Mary Quant lipstick radio, Temin is obsessed with the relationship between intimacy and difference. Associating and distancing, she draws the viewer in close to scrutinise her obsessions. Simultaneously she renounces that intimacy by placing her personal items in a large vitrine that stands in one of the most fetishised sites for outfitting the home: Conran's Habitat, an up market homestore. The desire to reveal herself through her possessions pulls you in while the commercial context and the institutional vitrine push you away.

In contrast to the idea of the monument, the collection always reflects the direct experience of the collector. Attempting to control his or her environment, the collector selects objects that reflect his or her own memory and obsessions. The monument externalises and generalises while the role of the collection is to focus and personalise. The need to control comes from a sense that something has gone out of control. Constantly mediating Temin navigates through the debris of memory classifying sensual, historical and psychological experience. She builds structures to contain, preserve and display an environment of emotional memory.

Yvette Brackman

Yvette Brackman is an artist who recently exhibited her work in Berlin with the curatorial collective Halte für Kunst. She has shown pieces at Up and Co. (NY), Greene Naftali Gallery (NY) and was included in the Video Library at David Zwirner (NY). Her work is also included in The Third Sculpture, a travelling exhibition curated by Ben Kinmont for Independent Curators Inc.. She has written for Frieze, Very, Zing and is a frequent contributor to Time Out New York.

Verde por fuera, roja por dentro
(Green on the Outside, Red on the Inside), 1993

Meyer Vaisman

"...you will come upon a house the entrance to which is completely
barricaded. Holly bushes obstruct the doorway, rough boards conceal
the windows below; while the casements of the upper stories are
neither closed nor open: for all the window frames are barred, but
the glass is broken...The chimneys are cracked, the roof is falling
in; as much of the rooms as can be seen from without presents a
dismantled appearance. The woodwork is rotten; the stone
mildewed...Such houses are considered haunted. The devil visits
them at night.

Houses are like the human beings who inhabit them. They become
to their former selves what the corpse is to the living body."

Victor Hugo, *Les Travailleurs de la mer*, in *Oeuvres complètes*.
Roman III, Paris: Robert Laffont, 1985, p. 50

How can home be mass-produced; or what culture has dropped along the way?[1]

For this new commission, Meyer Vaisman looked to the row of Phoenix temporary prefabs in Birmingham's Wake Green Road (recently given listing status). What remains of this initial reference in the resulting work is now little more than an echo embedded in the gallery wall.

The artist is no stranger to the make-shift constructions prefabs can appear to be. In 1995, having been elected to represent Venezuela at the Venice Biennale, he withdrew at the suggestion that his work be censored. Consisting of two structures, *Verde por fuera, roja por dentro*, and an Indian palafitos, they were not felt to represent the country with the dignity it required.

This experience has marked a change in mood in Vaisman's work from his earlier ironic pieces to these more recent autobiographical structures which can be read as questioning notions of permanence/impermanence, the monumental/mundane, machined/crafted and the cultural relativity of such concepts.

Pre-fabs are no strangers to art galleries. When the first prototypes were available for inspection by local government officials, they were erected in the grounds of the Tate Gallery in London. During the great wave of celebration for the 50th anniversary of VE Day in 1995, the prefab was used time and again as an icon for post-war peace and reconstruction in galleries and museums up and down the country.

It is appropriate then that in Vaisman's own Caracas boyhood home, recreated in recent pieces, one of the items seen through the peep-holes were chronicles of World War II. Such privileged access is now denied us in this latest piece. As he said last year in reference to the method of "reverse archaeology" which he employs in creating the rooms, his future work was likely to be "...totally impenetrable".

The meaning of the prefab is now largely lost to us, their serious purpose undercut by their cuteness. Amidst the current nostalgia for the 156,623 produced between 1945 and 1948, the hatred, or at best ambivalence, towards them as modern slums in the making has now largely disappeared. Yet they

Pre-Fab house 1998
Photo: Ashley Coombes/The Times.
Courtesy Pat & Tom Attenborrow

also offered the Modernist dream of the factory-made house that Le Courbusier sought in his dictum that a "house is a machine for living in". But the dream became a nightmare in the prefabs' appropriation of reactionary imagery and domestic detail - a front porch, your own garden and pitched roof. The functional was subverted by the small-scale symbolic in the name of instant domesticity.

Of the eleven or so different types of prefab some have lasted better than others, but having been designed to last only ten years, the wonder is that they have survived at all. Like childhood bedrooms that linger intact a while after we have left our parental home, they usually succumb to gradual alteration.

Where prefabs have survived, they have also changed as local authorities have re-clad and up-graded them. "Right-to-buy" policies have encouraged the stamp of individuality and private ownership to be further teased out of this mass-produced form of a home. We now have prefabs re-clad in the whole panoply of revivalist styles - mock-Tudor, neo-Georgian, executive classical, hacienda and even extending to two-storey.

Where Vaisman, in his concerns with the make-shift, and the shanty, also connects with the prefab is their after-life. They are re-used for garages, barns, cabbage dressing huts in the middle of fields, cricket pavilions, football changing rooms, summer houses, home offices, garden sheds, and even stables for very small ponies. Their parts litter the immemorial landscape of the allotment.

The canonical view of architectural history places the prefab fairly low down in the pecking order of important building types, if at all. Rarely, if ever, does it consider a building's use or abandonment. Conception and creation is privileged over use and abuse, the permanent over the temporary.

Lamenting the changes to the landscape of England since 1914, the historian W.G. Hoskins extolled the readers of his classic 1955 study "The Making of the English Landscape" to "turn away and contemplate the past before all is lost to the vandal". Amongst the violations he included "the Nissen hut, the prefab and the electric fence".

Green on the Outside, Red on the Inside
(My Parents' Closet) Minnesota Ice Fishin' House 1997 detail,
mixed-media installation, dimensions variable, Courtesy the artist.
Photo: Dan Dennehy, Courtesy Walker Art Center, Minneapolis

The prefab may be a "machine for living in", but as Frank Lloyd Wright's rejoinder has it "only in so far as the heart of a man is a suction pump".

Julian Holder

Notes
1. Part of the title is a reference to David A. Greene's claim that "Art no longer plays the role of the avant-garde...so much as it represents what culture has dropped along the way, or is in the act of neglecting", *Art & the Home*, Art & Design, Nov-Dec, 1996

Julian Holder teaches Architectural History and Conservation at University College, Chester and is a regular contributor to architectural magazines. Between 1993-95, he was consultant to English Heritage on its post-war thematic survey with particular responsibility for pre-fabs.

Carrie Mae Weems

Islands of Identity

"The Gullah Islands lie off the coast of South Carolina and Georgia. In the early eighteenth century, European transatlantic slave-traders brought thousands of West Coast Africans to these low coastal islands to work rice and cotton plantations. Isolated from the southern mainland and comprising a black majority, slaves of the Gullah Islands constructed patterns of everyday life and language rich in customs, languages, and lore of Africa. Contact with European and American cultures also made their lives a rich synthesis of practices and beliefs.

But since the society of the islands was structured in dominance, with English as the official language of slaveholding law and labour, the rich diversity, the syncretism of Gullah culture and its African provenance were often ignored or misinterpreted by men interested exclusively in white financial profit. Rather than seeing the islands as a place where the very word American was seasoned with deeply rooted African connotations, the islands were often interpreted by official folklore, anthology, religion, and linguistics merely as strongholds of an articulate black primitivism...

Sea Island Series
(hat on bed/shoes under bed) 1992
2 silver prints, edition of 10, 20 x 20" each
Photo: Courtesy PPOW, New York

If your lover tells you you're pretty and seems honest,
If your lover dotes constantly according to myth,
If your palm tells you you're tall with money,
If your road talks are leaded in meetings, and
If your tea-leaves and no-doubts are done a reliance that doesn't try,
If your final tarot constantly put knives in going to die,
If your tarot your cards in the free you'll never land neither,
If you fit your other fire glory red adheres to the time.

If a certain comes to your home and you never call his fire, and tell a
pan of water and place his preservance, lake trouble, and since it. If
somebody tells is upon and no not say to either go and see some the
in newspaper on a bay, do a string around a pot throw it in the river.
The leaves will return the pot to the sender. In a league make any place
turns in the water, sprinkle a line at noon, at your seven. The way's go
keep a nnoshe inwater secure, they're good for digging up measure
lines and other depot of many little, burled under your mattress. If
the time cannot shed and wears for burned you could the it smashed
up and perhaps to basis for loss.

A night and flying smoke your path unspoiled cold ambsy
has times be cold all in course on the ground. A rabbit
running across the grain maison moves ahead.

It's bad luck to turn back after starting out on a trip.
But if you dir, make a cross on the ground to keep away bad luck.

A rooster crowing just before midnight brings bad luck
when the flay a special three is own.

Sea Island Series
(woman in white/ pan of water), 1992
2 silver prints, 2 text panels
edition of 10, 20 x 20" each
Photo: Courtesy PPOW, New York

Products of West Africa in its New World etymologies, the first men and women were founders of the Gullah Islands. They emerged from fetid holds of European slaveships stunned. They were defined by the official language and law as chattel personal, no different from household furniture or barnyard oxen. They performed slave labour for white profit.

From the beginning, these deported women and men were the majority on these islands. Heat, humidity, malaria killed whites faster than the eye could blink. A black majority in these islands becoming Africa.

Not Africa in exile. Not Diaspora. These islands reflect Africa in stark single houses for slave habitation. Huts of the Americas, these houses are now angled and magisterial among trees. The house depicted in this exhibition is stone among wood. It is barely open to wind and light. A bare floor inside, redolent of earth and dark labour. Meagre belongings, cooking smoke, too many bodies at rest and in motion. But the house is inside, security, place of black family rituals. It is the centre of the Slave Community, an African nation in miniature, rising among strong trees..."

Extracts from Houston A. Baker Jr.,"Islands of Identity: Inside the Pictures of Carrie Mae Weems", *In these Islands: South Carolina and Georgia by Carrie Mae Weems*, University of Alabama, Sarah Moody Gallery of Art, Tuscaloosa, Alabama, 1994. Houston A. Baker Jr. is an English Professor and Director of the Center for the Study of Black Literature and Culture at the University of Pennsylvania. His most recent published work is *Black Studies, Rap and the Academy* (University of Chicago Press).

THE
HOUSE

When you move into
a new house, remove old
spirits by washing around the windows and doors with vinegar water. But,
prevent spirits from crossing the doorstep by
putting salt and pepper along the door and window sills.

Trimming the windows in blue will ward off hags,
witches and other evil spirits.

Wall paper your home with newspaper. Before a hag can bother
you, it must read every word. And if it can't read, then there you go.
But newspaper strung between an antenna will do the job too.

Place rice in the four corners of your home for good luck and
put a glass of water in a corner to absorb evil spirits.

A kitchen knife stuck into the wood over the door will keep
witches out of the house when the family is away.

If you swept dust out of the house at sunset you just might sweep away
the spirit of a family member.

Never build an addition to your house. A home can never be extended.

Sea Island Series (house) 1992
3 silver prints, 1 text panel, each panel 20 x 20",
Collection of Eileen and Peter Norton, Santa Monica.
Photo: Courtesy PPOW, New York

Rachel Whiteread

dolce domum

"Memory, childhood experiences, staging the scenes of origins and endings, these are fundamental themes that run through Whiteread's work: spaces of concealment (she recalls an early memory of hiding in a cupboard), of sexuality and death - mattresses, baths, mortuary slabs, the home as the site of memory and our formative experiences. Simple objects reveal ambiguities that shift their identity and introduce an element of uncertainty. Invested with shared meanings - the functions of the body, familial experience, the patterns of everyday life - they are sufficiently strange to evade the closure that accompanies classification, like a memory trace that hovers at the edge of recall, or the moment of waking when a dream image slips out of consciousness to leave a residue of uneasiness and intrigue.

The implied referent for Whiteread's sculptures became explicit in (the art work) *House* as the cultural space of the home, an identifiable place and place of identity. The home represents a key component in the constitution of identity, a point of reference amongst the shifting patterns of our social and cultural formation, a focus for desires and longings, a point of origin and return, the universal experience of acquiring a place in the world. The home is the context for initiating social relations, a microcosm of all possible worlds and the

Untitled (Torso) 1992
dental plaster, 10 x 22.9 x 7.2 cm
copy no. 9, edition of 12, Private Collection, London
Photo: Mike Bruce,
Courtesy Anthony d'Offay Gallery, London

space in which we make our first differentiation between interiority and exteriority and learn to distinguish between safety and danger, pleasure and pain, desire and gratification...

The house is the primary unit of measurement and point of reference for a spatial politics, a human scale which determines the nature of our relationship to the immediate environment and beyond that to the culture as a whole. "Where do you live?" figures amongst the key questions which momentarily arrest the narratives of identity, how we answer determining our place within a grid of co-ordinates which plot social subjectivity. Homelessness begs the issue of where home might actually be. The common experience of the homeless and the migrant is to be made to feel out of place. Home not only becomes the mythical point of origin (the fundamental question every child asks the parent - "Where did I come from?") but also a utopian projection, a homeland. Home is a fiction, a concept we carry around with us, our narrative of identity and (be)longing: 'For our house is our corner of the world...it is our first universe, a real cosmos in every sense of the word.'[1]

Childhood is the period when the boundaries between self and other, body and space, inside and outside, are in the process of formation. Children constantly make places (dens or tents) to discover places within the house for solitude or escape - from parental authority, sibling rivalry, unwanted friends - utilising cupboards, wardrobes, beds; the marginal spaces underneath, between, inside the object world. The representation in dreams of a desire for invisibility (hiding or being unfindable) is seen by Freud as an intimation of mortality - 'another unmistakable symbol of death'.[2] These discoveries - of edges, borders, boundaries, inside and outside, visibility and invisibility - are all recurrent activities that possess particular significance (symbolic meanings) during childhood, providing the template for experiences in adult life...

Whiteread's works are very much about surface and the significance of the detail. Their three-dimensional facticity does

Untitled (Air Bed II) 1992
rubber & neoprene, 22 x 120 x 194 cm
Collection Tate Gallery, London.
Photo: Courtesy Anthony d'Offay Gallery, London

not primarily function as spatial division but reinforces surface:
a surface for inscription. Despite Minimalist allusions her
works do not emphasise an 'objecthood' that implicates the
viewer's bodily presence but, rather, the absent body. The
spectral presence of the body haunts the work as surface details
offer enigmatic clues to the repetitive and mundane acts of
everyday life. What disturbs meaning in Whiteread's work...
is the psychopathology that lies beneath the everyday; the
repressed fears, desires, prohibitions and transgressions that lurk
within the social routines as the uncanny stalks the familiar, and
the inanimate threatens to come alive."

Notes
1 Gaston Bachelard, *The Poetics of Space*, trans. Maria Jolas, Beacon Press, 1969, p. 70
2 Sigmund Freud, "The Three Caskets", *Standard Edition*, Vol. XII

Extracts from Jon Bird, "dolce domum", *Rachel Whiteread: house*, Phaidon Press Ltd.,
1995, p. 112, 119, 121 and 124. Jon Bird is Professor in Art & Critical Theory,
Middlesex University, writer and curator.

LIST OF WORKS IN THE EXHIBITION

HOWARD ARKLEY

Deluxe Setting, 1992, acrylic on canvas, 173 x 135cm,
Collection Brian & Kalli Rolfe, Melbourne
Interior Tableau, 1992, acrylic on canvas, 173 x 135cm,
Private Collection, Melbourne

UTA BARTH

Untitled (98.5), 1998, edition of 5, triptych of colour photographs, 38" x 197.5",
Commissioned by Ikon Gallery for *Claustrophobia*
Ground #66, 1996, colour photograph, 19.5" x 20.5"
Ground #52, 1995, colour photograph, 9.75" x 12"
Ground #35, 1994, colour photograph, 19.5" x 20.5"
Ground #78, 1997, colour photograph, 41" x 39"
Courtesy London Projects, London

MARK BENNETT

Home of Herman and Lily Munster, 1986-95, ink and pencil on graph vellum paper,
24" x 36" sheet, Private Collection, Connecticut
Home of the Cunninghams, 1995, ink and pencil on graph vellum paper,
24" x 36" sheet, Collection Eric Mellencamp, Seal Beach, California
Home of Bruce Wayne and Dick Grayson, Gotham City, 1997, ink and pencil
on graph vellum paper, 24" x 36" sheet, Collection Hilarie and Mark Moore,
Orange, California

JAMES CASEBERE

*Fork in the Refrigerato*r, 1975, silver gelatin print unmounted, 12" x 14" framed,
Collection of the artist
Golden Apple, 1986, silver gelatin print framed on museum board, 40" x 50"
framed, Collection of the artist
Nine Alcoves, 1995, dye destruction print - base mounted to plexi, 48" x 48"
Collection of the artist. Courtesy: Lisson Gallery, London

MAT COLLISHAW

Enchanted Wardrobe, 1994, wooden wardrobe, 225 x 130 x 70cm,
Collezione Re Rebaudengo Sandretto, Torino

CAROLYN ESKDALE

Untitled Room 6.98, 1998, installation, approx. 185 x 370cm
Commissioned by Ikon Gallery for *Claustrophobia*

MELANIE FRIEND

Homes and Gardens
Documenting the Invisible: Images of Kosovo, 1994-5
six photographs, 35.5 x 35.5cm each and soundtrack, Collection of the artist.
Edited from a series of sixteen photographs originally shown at Camerawork,
London, Summer 1996

MONA HATOUM

Doormat, 1996, stainless steel pins, nickel-plated pins, glue, canvas, 1996, 3 x 71
x 40.5cm, Collection of the artist

PERMINDAR KAUR

The Silent Partner, 1998 steel bed, wooden box, light, approx. 250 x 250cm
Commissioned by Ikon Gallery for *Claustrophobia*
Living the Waking World Asleep, 1998
steel beds intervention in loft apartment in Birmingham
Commissioned by Ikon Gallery for *Claustrophobia*

MATTHIAS MÜLLER

Home Stories, 1990, (video - duration 6 mins), Collection of the artist

DORIS SALCEDO

Untitled (cement cabinet), 1995, wood, cement, glass, steel, 162 x 99.5 x 37cm, Caldic Collectie, Rotterdam

NINA SAUNDERS

Forever, 1998, swing, wooden panels, wallpaper, soundtrack, compressor mechanism, approx. 250 x 250cm
Commissioned by Ikon Gallery for *Claustrophobia*

KATHY TEMIN

Indoor Monument: A Monument to the Home (in the rumpus room video), 1995-8
TV monitor, picnic box, video
Collection of the artist.
Courtesy Anna Schwartz Gallery, Melbourne

MEYER VAISMAN

Untitled, 1998, installation, cement bricks, door frame
Commissioned by Ikon Gallery for *Claustrophobia*

CARRIE MAE WEEMS

Sea Island Series (house), 1992, 3 silver prints, 1 text panel, each panel 20" x 20", Collection of Eileen and Peter Norton, Santa Monica
Sea Island Series (hat on bed/shoes under bed), 1992, 2 silver prints, edition of 10, 20" x 20" each, Collection of the artist. Courtesy PPOW, New York
Sea Island Series (woman in white/pan of water), 1992, 2 silver pints, 2 text panels, 20" x 20" each, Collection of the artist. Courtesy PPOW, New York

RACHEL WHITEREAD

Untitled (Air Bed II), 1992, rubber & neoprene, 22 x 120 x 194cm, Collection Tate Gallery, London. Purchased with assistance from the Patrons of New Art through the Tate Gallery Foundation, 1993 (note: only on exhibition at Ikon Gallery)
Untitled (Torso), 1992, dental plaster, 10 x 22.9 x 7.2cm, copy no. 9, edition of 12, Private Collection, London

BIOGRAPHIES

HOWARD ARKLEY

Born 1951, Melbourne, Australia
Lives and works in Melbourne, Australia

Selected solo exhibitions since 1990
1997 *Spray: The Work of Howard Arkley*, Tolarno Galleries, Melbourne
1995 *White + Black: 20 years work on paper and canvas*, Tolarno Galleries, Melbourne
1994 *The Pointilist Suburb Series*, Tolarno Galleries, Melbourne
1992 *Mix n' Match*, Tolarno Galleries, Melbourne
1991 *HA: Howard Arkley (retrospective)*, Monash University Gallery, Melbourne
     Blue Chip Instant Decorator: A Room, in collaboration with Juan Davila, Tolarno Galleries, Melbourne
1990 *The Head Show*, Tolarno Galleries, Melbourne

Selected group exhibitions since 1993
1996 *Into and Out of Abstraction*, National Gallery of Victoria, Melbourne
     Compost, Adelaide Festival, Adelaide, South Australia
     Familiar and Strange: Australian Contemporary Art, Seoul Arts Center, Korea
     Contemporary Australia: Six Leading Artists, United Overseas Bank, Singapore
1995 *Downtown: Ruscha, Rooney, Arkley*, Museum of Modern Art at Heide
1993 *The John McCaughey Memorial Art Prize*, National Gallery of Victoria
     Beyond the Surface, Dick Butt Gallery, Hobart
     High Pop, Roslyn Oxley9 Gallery, Sydney

Selected bibiography since 1992
Crawford, Ashley and Edgar, Ray, *Spray: The Work of Howard Arkley*, A World Art Book, Craftsman House, NSW, 1997
Gibson, Jeff, "Los Melbos", *Art + Text*, 1995, pp. 20-21
Gregory, John, *Mix n' Match,* (catalogue), Tolarno Galleries, Melbourne, 1992
McAuliffe, Chris, *Art & Suburbia*, Craftsman House, NSW, 1996
Morrell, Timothy, *Australia Familiar & Strange* (catalogue), The Asialink Centre of the University of Melbourne, 1996
Nelson, Robert, "That Suburban Something", *The Age*, Saturday Extra, Sept. 22 1995
Rooney, Robert, "Turning Suburbia Inside Out", *The Australian*, Nov. 21, 1992

UTA BARTH

Born 1958, Berlin, Germany
Lives and works in Los Angeles, California

Selected solo exhibitions since 1995
1998 Tanya Bonakdar Gallery, New York
London Projects, London
ACME, Los Angeles
Lawing Gallery, Houston, Texas
1997 *The Wall Project*, Museum of Contemporary Art, Chicago:
Andrehn-Schiptjenko, Stockholm, Sweden
Rena Bransten Gallery, San Francisco, California
1996 Tanya Bonakdar Gallery, New York
London Projects, London
SL Simpson Gallery, Toronto
1995 Museum of Contemporary Art, Los Angeles, California (catalogue)

Selected group exhibitions since 1996
1998 *Mysterious Voyages: Exploring the Subject of Photography*, Contemporary Museum,
Baltimore, Maryland
(Not Pictured) The Presence of Absence, The Light Factory, Charlotte, NC
1997 *Heart, Mind, Body, Soul: American Art in the 1990s*, Whitney Museum of
American Art, New York
Object and Abstraction: Contemporary Photography, Museum of Modern Art, NY
Blueprint, De Appel, Amsterdam (catalogue)
Painting into Photography/Photography into Painting, Museum of Contemporary
Art, Miami (catalogue)
Evidence: Photography and Site, Wexner Center for the Arts, Columbus, Ohio
1996 *Painting - The Extended Field*, Rooseum Center for Contemporary Art, Malmö
Light . Time . Focus, Museum of Contemporary Photography, Chicago
Extended Minimal, Max Protech, New York

Selected bibliography since 1996
Browning, Simon, Mack, Michael, Perkins, Sean, *Surface: Contemporary Photographic Practice*, Booth-Clibborn Editions, 1997, p. 236
Conkelton, Sheryl, "Uta Barth", *Journal of Contemporary Art*, Vol. 8.1, Summer 97
Kim, Soo Jin, "Uta Barth: Project", *Art & The Home*, Art & Design, Winter 1996, pp. 48-57
Koeniger, Kay, "Photographs document human places mostly by leaving people out", *The Columbus Dispatch*, March 23 1996
Pagel, David, "Inside Jobs: Portraits of Interiors", *The Los Angeles Times*, August 1 1997
Rugoff, Ralph, *Scene of the Crime*, ex. cat., essays by Antony Vidler and Peter Wollen, MIT Press, 1997, p. 169

MARK BENNETT

Born 1956, Chattanooga, Tennessee
Lives and works in Los Angeles, California

Selected solo exhibitions since 1996
1999 University of Tennessee, Chattanooga
1998 *Teleburbia*, Augen Gallery, Portland, Oregon
1997 Mark Moore Gallery, Santa Monica, California
     Corcoran Gallery of Art, Washington D.C. and touring US
     Fantasy TV Blueprints, Orange County Museum of Art, Newport Beach, CA
1996 Huntington Beach Art Center, Huntington Beach

Selected group exhibitions since 1995
1998 *Inventory*, White Columns, New York
     Tune In, Lawing Gallery, Houston, Texas
     Triennial, Phoenix Art Museum, Phoenix, Arizona
1997 *To be Real*, Center for the Arts, Yerba Buena Gardens, San Francisco
     The Road Show, Bronwyn Keenan Gallery, New York
1996 *Happy Days*, Contemporary Arts Center, Cincinnati, Ohio
     Location, Location, San José Institute of Contemporary Art, San José
     Nirvana: Capitalism and the Consumed Image, Center of Contemporary Art,
     Seattle, Washington
1995 *Hostile Witness*, Washington Project for the Arts (WPA), Washington D.C.

Selected public collections
Los Angeles County Museum of Art, CA
University of Colorado, Boulder
Orange County Museum of Art, Newport Beach, CA

Selected Bibliography
Anon., "Mark Bennett", *Art & The Home*, Art & Design, No. 51, 1996, pp. 33-37
Clark, Champ, "Dream Houses: Mark Bennett's obsession with make-believe TV
homes turns into a blueprint for success", *People Magazine*, February 17, 1997
Crain, Mary Beth, "And I Shall Dwell in the House of the TV Forever", *L.A.
Weekly*, December 8-14 1995, p. 68
Hickson, Kathryn, "Clarity", *New Art Examiner*, May 1996, pp. 42-43
Pagel, David, "Mark Bennett at Mark Moore Gallery", *Artissues*, No. 42,
March/April 1996, p. 43

JAMES CASEBERE

Born 1953, Lansing, Michigan, USA
Lives and works in New York, USA

Selected solo exhibitions since 1995
1998 Sean Kelly Gallery, New York
    Galerie Tanit, Munich, Germany
1997 Jean Bernier, Athens, Greece
    Williams College Museum of Art, Williamstown
1996-7 The Ansel Adas Center for Photography, San Francisco
1996 Lisson Gallery, London
1995 Michael Klein inc., New York

Selected group exhibitions since 1994
1998 *Where: Allegories of Site in Contemporary Art*, Whitney Museum of American
    Art at Champion, Stamford, CT
1997 *Architecture as Metaphor*, Museum of Modern Art, New York
    Selections from the Permanent Collection, The Whitney Museum of American
    Art, New York
    Elsewhere, The Carnegie Museum of Art, Pittsburgh, PA
1995 *Campo*, Venice Biennale, Venice, Italy (travelled to Torino, Italy and
    Konstmuseum, Malmö, Sweden 1996
    Prison Sentences: The Prison at Site/The Prison as Subject, Eastern Pennsylvania
    State Penitentiary, Philadelphia, PA
1994 *House Rules*, Wexner Center for the Visual Arts, Columbus, OH

Selected bibliography
Batchen, Geoffrey, "James Casebere's Prison Series", *Creative Camera*, June/July
1996, p.14-21
Berke, Deborah and Harris, Steven, eds., *Architecture of the Everyday*, Princeton
Architectural Press, 1998
Berger, Maurice, essay and Grundberg, Andy, intro., *James Casebere: Model Culture,
Photographs, 1975-1996*, Friends of Photography, San Francisco
Crump, James, "Solitary Spaces", *Art in America*, October 1997, pp. 57-59
Hagen, Charles, "James Casebere", *New York Times*, April 14 1995, p. C14
Hall, Jacqueline, "New Angles on 'Home': 90s Domestic Spaces Analyzed,
Challenged by Varied Ideologies", *Columbus Dispatch*, September 18 1994
House Rules, special issue of *Assemblage*, MIT Press Journal 1994
Ziolkowski, Thad, "James Casebere: Michael Klein Gallery", *Artforum*, September
1995

MAT COLLISHAW

Born 1966, Nottingham, England
Lives and works in London, England

Selected solo exhibitions since 1995

1998 Bloom Gallery, Amsterdam
1997 Lisson Gallery, London
  Ideal Boys, Ridinghouse Editions, London, Gallerie Analix, Geneva
1996 Tanya Bonakdar Gallery, New York
1995 Galerie Analix, Geneva
  Karsten Schubert, London (in collaboration with Thomas Dane)
  Camden Arts Centre, London

Selected group exhibitions since 1995

1998 *Close Echoes*, City Gallery, Prague
  Exterminating Angel, Galerie Ghislaine Hussenot, Paris
1997 *Live/Life*, Fundaçao des Descobertas, Lisbon, Portugal
  Urban Legends, Staatliche Kunsthalle Baden Baden, Germany
  Sensation, Royal Academy of Arts, London
  Pictura Britannica, Museum of Contemporary Art, Sydney
1996 *More than Real*, Palazzo Reale Caserta, Naples
  Hybrids, De Appel, Amsterdam
  Manifesta, Natural History Museum, Rotterdam (catalogue)
  The Inner Eye, Manchester City Art Gallery (catalogue)
  Digital Gardens, The Power Plant, Toronto
  Live/Life, Musée d'Art Moderne, Paris (catalogue)
  Exchanging Interiors, Museum van Loon, Amsterdam
1995 *Corpus Delicti - London in the 90s*, Kunstforeningen, Copenhagen (cat.)
  Wild Walls, Stedelijk Museum, Amsterdam (catalogue)
  Brilliant: New Art from London, Walker Art Centre, Minneapolis (catalogue)
  British Art Show 4, Manchester, Edinburgh, Cardiff (catalogue)
  Instanbul Biennale III

Selected bibliography

Cork, Richard, "If you go down to the woods today...", *The Times*, London, December 2 1997
Hall, James, "Mat Collishaw: Lisson Gallery", *Artforum*, No. 5, January 1998, pp. 111-112
Herbert, Martin, "The Mechanics of Seduction", *Dazed and Confused*, Issue 23, August 1996
Maloney, Martin, "Mat Collishaw, Karsten Schubert, Camden Arts Centre", *Artforum*, April 1996
Morrissey, Simon, "Interrogating Beauty", *Contemporary Visual Arts*, Issue 16, 1997, pp. 26-33

CAROLYN ESKDALE

Born 1963, Bendigo, Victoria, Australia
Lives and works in Melbourne, Australia

Selected solo exhibitions since 1994
1997 *Drawings*, Temple Studio, Melbourne
    Untitled Room 4.97, Pendulum, Sydney
1996 *Untitled Room 8.96*, Temple Studio, Melbourne
1995 *Drawings*, Ether Ohnetitel, Melbourne
    the untitled room 8.95, Building 40 Project, RMIT, Melbourne
1994 *Reconstructed Furniture*, Temple Studio, Melbourne

Selected group exhibitions since 1994
1998 *All This and Heaven Too*, Adelaide Biennial of Australian Art, Art Gallery of
    South Australia, Adelaide
1997 *Moët & Chandon Exhibition*, Brisbane (touring)
1996 *Location, Location, Location*, Linden Gallery, Melbourne
    Rapport, Singapore Art Museum, Monash University Gallery, Melbourne
    Mrs Bird's House, Motherwell St., Melbourne
    Secret Archive, Platform 2, Degraves St. Subway, Melbourne
    Cut Outs, Stop 22, Melbourne
1994 *43 Countries, 75 Artists*, Cité Internationale des Arts, Paris
    The Aberrant Object - Women, Dada and Surrealism, Museum of Modern
    Art at Heide, Melbourne

Public collections
National Gallery of Victoria, Melbourne
City of Port Philip Collection
Bendigo Regional Art Gallery

Bibliography
Creed, Barbara, "The Aberrant Object: Women, Dada and Surrealism", *Art Monthly*, May 1994, p.10
Engberg, Juliana, "A Cabinet of Curiosities", *The Aberrant Object*, exhibition catalogue, Museum of Modern Art at Heide, Melbourne, March 1994
Ludeman, Brenda, "Assembling the Familial Archive", ex. cat., *All This and Heaven Too*, Adelaide Biennial of Australian Art, Art Gallery of South Australia, 1998
Ludeman, Brenda, "The Fabric of Fiction", Globe -
http:/www.arts.monash.edu.au/visarts/globe/ghome.html, 1997
King, Natalie, *Rapport*, Monash University & Singapore Art Museum, June 1996
McAuliffe, Chris, "Pull up a Chair", *World Art*, Vol. 1, No. 2, 1994
Moore, Ross, "Decking out identities - performing gender", *Art Monthly*, June 1994
Webb, Penny "Carolyn Eskdale - Reconstructed Furniture", *Agenda*, #36, May 1994

MELANIE FRIEND

Born 1957, London, England
Lives in London, England

Melanie Friend is a freelance photojournalist whose work has been published in magazines and newspapers including The Guardian, The Independent, The New York Times, Marie-Claire, New Statesman & Society and War Report. Her recent work has focused on the Balkans.

Selected solo exhibitions
1996-9 *Homes and Gardens*, Camerawork, London and touring UK and
      Houston, USA (catalogue)
1988-90 *Mothers' Pride*, Spectrum Festival, London, F-stop Gallery, Bath &
      Cambridge Darkroom

Selected group exhibitions
1994   XX Art, London
1991-3 *Silent Health*, Camerawork, London, touring UK and Ireland
1991   *Mothers and Daughters*, Watershed, Bristol and touring UK

Radio
Features for the BBC including:
A Passion for Bulgaria, Radio 4, 1994
Inside Kosovo, BBC Radio 4, 1992

Part-time lecturer at the London College of Printing & University of Humberside

MONA HATOUM

Born 1952, Beirut, Lebanon
Lives and works in London, England since 1975

Selected solo exhibitions since 1995

1998 Museum of Modern Art, Oxford
1997-8 Museum of Contemporary Art, Chicago and New Museum of
 Contemporary Art, New York
 Galerie Rene Blouin, Montreal
1996 Gallery Anadiel, Jerusalem
 The Fabric Workshop and Museum, Philadelphia
 Current Disturbance, Capp Street Project, San Francisco
 Quarters, Via Farini, Milan
 De Appel, Amsterdam
1995 *Socle du Monde*, White Cube/Jay Jopling, London
 Short Space, Galerie Chantal Crousel, Paris
 Mona Hatoum, British School in Rome

Selected group exhibitions since 1995

1998 *Real Life: New British Art*, British Council Touring Exhibition, Japan
1997 *Sensation*, Royal Academy of Arts, London
 History: Image-based work in Britain in the late 20th Century, Ferens Art
 Gallery, Kingston-upon-Hull, and UK tour
 Material Culture: The Object in British Art of the 80s and 90s, Hayward Gallery,
 London
1996 *Life/Live* Musée d'art moderne de la Ville de Paris, Paris:
 Inclusion/Exclusion, Steirischer Herbst, Graz, Austria
 Inside the Visible, ICA, Boston,
 Distemper: Dissonant Themes in the Art of the 90s, Hirschorn Museum and
 Sculpture Garden, Washington
 NowHere, Louisiana Museum of Modern Art, Humlebaek, Denmark
1995 *Rites of Passage*, Tate Gallery, London
 The Turner Prize Exhibition, Tate Gallery, London

Selected bibliography

Anson, Libby, "Mona Hatoum: White Cube", *Art Monthly*, March 1995,
pp. 52-53
Archer, Michael, "Mona Hatoum: Mario Flecha", *Artforum* 31, no.2, December
1992, pp. 107-8
Shapira, Sarit, "Mona Hatoum: Anadiel", *Flash Art* 20, no. 190, October 1996,
pp. 121-22
Stathatos, John, "Mona Hatoum", *Art Monthly*, no. 129, September 1989, p. 16
Walker, Caryn Faure, "Mona Hatoum", *Art Monthly*, no. 164, March 1993,
p. 22-23

PERMINDAR KAUR

Born 1965, Nottingham, England
Lives and works in London, England

Selected solo exhibitions since 1993
1998 *Independent Thoughts*, Castle Museum & Art Gallery, Norwich
1997 *Secrets must Circulate*, Galeria Carles Poy, Barcelona
1996 *Cold Comfort I*, Ikon Gallery, Birmingham
     Cold Comfort II, Mead Gallery, Warwick Arts Centre, Coventry
1995 *Small Spaces*, Galleri Isidor, Malmö, Sweden
1994 *Hidden Witnesses*, Galleri Amidol, Gothenurg
1993 *Red Earth*, Harris Museum and Art Gallery, Preston

Selected group exhibitions since 1995
1998 *Where I am*, Galeria da Mitra, Lisbon, as part of Caminho do Oriente,
     Expo '98
1997 *Flexible Co-existence*, Art Tower Mito, Mito, Japan
     Krishna: The Divine Lover, National Touring Exhibitions, Whitechapel Art
     Gallery, London and UK tour
     Las Ninas de Mis Ojos, Galeria Trajeeto, Vitoria, Spain
     Pictura Britannica - Art from Britain, Museum of Contemporary Art, Sydney
     Crosscurrents, University Museum of Ethnography, Oslo
     Out of India, Queens Museum of Art, New York
1996 *Falling*, Museu Salvador Vilaseca, Reus, Spain
1995 *Por al buit/miedo al vacio*, Galeria Carles Poy, Barcelona
     Veins, Galeria Dels Angels, Barcelona
     British Art Show 4, Manchester, Edinburgh, Cardiff

Selected bibliography
Andrews, Jorelle, "Re-negotiating the Familiar: Inhabiting the Strange: The
Installations of Permindar Kaur", *Crosscurrents*, Oslo Museum of Ethnography, 1997
Chambers, Eddie, "Cold Comfort", *Third Text 36*, Autumn 1996, pp. 91-96
Doherty, Claire, "While you were sleeping...", *Cold Comfort*, Ikon Gallery, 1996
Doherty, Claire, "Cold Comfort", *Transcript*, vol. 2, issue 2, p. 18-25
Juncosa, Enrique, "Las Nuevas Confesiones", *El Pais*, March 1994
Masterton, Piers, "Cold Comfort", *Art Monthly*, 198, July - August 1996,
pp. 33-34
Proctor, Nancy, "Is Women's Art Homeless", *Make 71*, August - Sept 1996,
p. 10-11

MATTHIAS MÜLLER

Born 1961, Bielefeld, Germany
Lives and works in Bielefeld, Germany.

Matthias Müller has been active as a filmmaker since 1980. In 1985 he co-founded the Alte Kinder film co-operative. Up to 1987, some of his films were co-directed with filmmaker Christiane Heuwinkel. Since 1984, Müller has collaborated with Berlin-based composer and musician Dirk Schaefer. Müller has organised numerous avant-garde film events for several institutions. He has curated and presented touring programmes of German experimental films in Germany, Belgium, the Netherlands, Finland, Great Britain, Lithuania, Hungary, Poland, France, Switzerland, Austria, Canada and the USA, occasionally in co-operation with the Goethe Insitute or the Filmbüro North Rhine-Westphalia.

International Film Festivals include Cannes, Berlin and New York.
Museum of Modern Art, New York, 1994

Film Awards for Home Stories, 1990
2nd Prize of the Jury and 3rd Prize of the Youth Jury, Odense International Film Festival, 1993
Targa Fedic, Mostra Internazionale di Montecatini Terme, 1992
Honorable Mention, Festival International du Jeune Cinema, Montreal, 1992
Honorable Mention, San Francisco International Film Festival, 1992
Prix de la Recherche, Festival du Court-Metrage, Clermont-Ferrand, 1992
Audience Award, Maritime Filmtage Wilhelmshaven, 1991
Millor Montatge, Badalona Film Festival, 1991
Preis der Deutschen Filmkritik, "Best German Short Film of the Year", Association of German Film Critics, 1991

Collections
Centre Georges Pompidou, Paris
Nederlands Film Museum, Amsterdam
Experimental Film Archive, Avignon
Korean Cinemathéque, Seoul
Universities of Hawaii, Boulder, Chicago, Frankfurt-am-Main

DORIS SALCEDO

Born 1958, Bogotá, Columbia
Lives and works in Bogotá, Columbia.

Selected solo exhibitions since 1994
1998 New Museum of Contemporary Art, New York; Site Santa Fe, Santa Fe,
1996 *Atrabiliarios*, LA Louver Gallery, Los Angeles
    Doris Salcedo, Le Creux de L'Enfer, Thiers, France
    Galeria Camargo Vilaca, Sao Paolo
1995 White Cube, London
1994 *La Casa Viuda*, Brooke Alexander, New York

Selected group exhibitions since 1996
1998 *From head to toe: concepts of the body in Twentieth-Century Art*, Los
    Angeles County Museum of Art, Los Angeles
    Displacements: Miroslaw Balka, Doris Salcedo, Rachel Whiteread, The Art
    Gallery of Ontario, Toronto
    Wounds: between democracy and redemption in contemporary art, Moderna
    Museet, Stockholm
1997 *Body*, The Art Gallery of New South Wales, Sydney
    Words and Images, Miami Art Museum, Miami
1996 *The Visible & the Invisible: representing the body in contemporary art and society*,
    Institute of International Visual Arts, St. Pancras, London
    Distemper: Dissonant Themes in the Art of the 1990s, The Hirshorn Museum and
    Sculpture Garden, Washington D.C. (catalogue)
    Dissonant Wounds: Zones of Display/Metaphors of Atrophy, Center for Curatorial
    Studies, Bard College, Annadale-on-Hudson

Selected bibliography
Adams, Brooks, "Domestic Globalism at the Carnegie", *Art in America*, 1996
Amor, Monica, "Doris Salcedo", *Art Nexus*, July-September 1994
Aukeman, Anastasia, "Privileged Position", *ARTnews*, March 1994
Bradley, Jessica, "Introduction" and Huyssen, Andreas, "Sculpture, Materiality and
Memory in the Age of America", *Displacements: Balka, Salcedo, Whiteread*, ex. cat.,
Art Gallery of Ontario, Toronto, 1998
Cambi, Leslie, "Last Supper", *The Village Voice XLIII*, no. 15, April 14 1998, p.125
Cameron, Dan, "Absence Makes the Art", *Artforum*, October 1994
Gomez, Edward M., "In the Afterlight of Bloodshed, Smoldering Images", *The New
York Times*, March 15, 1998, pp. 2-39
Guitierrez, Natalia, "Conversation with Doris Salcedo", *Art Nexus*, January-MßArch
1996
Merewether, Charles, "Doris Salcedo: The anonymity of violence: re-elaborating
the non-site", *Propositions*, ex. cat., 1998, pp. 102-106

NINA SAUNDERS

Born 1958, Odense, Denmark
Lives and works in London, England

Solo exhibitions
1996 *Hidden Agenda*, Bluecoat Gallery, Liverpool and
  Northern Gallery of Contemporary Art, Sunderland
1995 *Familiar Territories*, Ferens Art Gallery, Hull
  Priority Zone, Public Art Festival, Hull

Group Exhibitions
1998 *Fetish Show*, Art Gallery of Windsor, Canada
  Me and You, Walsall Museum and Art Gallery, Walsall
  Personal Effects: Sculpture and Belongings, Spacex, Exeter
1997-8 *Date with An Artist*, Northern Gallery of Contemporary Art, Sunderland
  and BBC
  Bittersweet, Whitworth Art Gallery, Manchester
1996 *Young British Artists*, Saatchi Gallery
  Sculpture in the Close, Quincentenary Exhibition, Jesus College, Cambridge
  Dansk Skulptur i 125 ar, Nordjyllands Kunstmuseum, Denmark
1995 *The London Group Biennial*, The Concourse Gallery, Barbican, London
1994 *Proms II*, Kunsthallen Brandts Klaederfabrik, Odense, Denmark
1993 *Confrontations*, Walsall Museum and Art Gallery, Worcester City Museum
  & Art Gallery and Untitled Gallery, Sheffield
  Visionfest 93, Money, Value & Exchange, London

Collections
Ferens Art Gallery, Hull
Private Collection, Lord Renfrew, Cambridge
Saatchi Collection
Walsall Museum and Art Gallery, West Midlands

Selected bibliography
"Arts Review", *The Guardian*, 13 March 1997
"Danish born artist brings feelings to the fabric of her work", *The Western Mail*,
August 1997
"Look, don't sit", *The Observer*, 6 April 1997
Barnett, P., "Purity and Fear", *Make Magazine*, February/March 1997
Jardine, L., "Pregnant with meaning", *Modern Painters*, Autumn 1997
Jardine, L., "It was only a white leather sofa", *The Guardian*, 1 October 1994
Kinsey Milner, R., "Impure Thoughts: Gendering Architectural Space", *Hidden
Agenda*, Bluecoat Gallery, 1996

KATHY TEMIN

Born 1968, Sydney, Australia
Currently living and working in New York, USA (Australia Council, PS1 studio)

Selected solo exhibitions since 1995

1998 *Kathy Temin*, Anna Schwartz Gallery, Melbourne
1997 *Some of my favourite things*, Habitat Store, Tottenham Court Road, London
     Cat Mat, Cleveland, London
1996 *Model Homes*, Roslyn Oxley 9 Gallery, Sydney
     Home Dis-Play, Anna Schwarz Gallery, Melbourne
1995 *New Work*, Galerie van Gelder, Amsterdam
     Wall drawings, Objects and Videos: Made in New Plymouth, Govett
     Brewster Art Gallery, New Zealand
     Three Indoor Monuments, Australian Centre for Contemporary Art,
     Melbourne

Selected group exhibitions since 1996

1998 *Inglenook*, Feigen Contemporary Art, New York
     Wish You Luck, PS1 Studio Program exhibition, PS1 NY
     Furnish, Bendigo Contemporary Art Gallery, Melbourne
1997 *The Seppelt Contemporary Art Award*, Museum of Contemporary Art,
     Sydney
     Humdrum, The Apartment, Coldharbour Lane, Brixton, London
     Strangely Familiar, Ikon Gallery, Birmingham, Touring Exhibition
     Thoughts, City Racing, London
1996 *Second Asia Pacific Triennial*, Queensland Art Gallery, Brisbane
     Manifesta 1., Villa Museumpark, Rotterdam
     Ruins in Reverse, RMIT Gallery, Storey Hall, Melbourne
     White Hysteria, Experimental Art Foundation, South Australia

Selected bibliography

Cass, Naomi, "Interview with Kathy Temin", *Three Indoor Monuments*, The
Australian Centre for Contemporary Art, Melbourne (catalogue), 1995
Coleman, Felicity, "Kathy Temin at Anna Schwartz Gallery", *Art/Text,* no.62, 98
Cramer, Sue, "Kathy Temin: Front", *HQ Magazine*, March 1998
James, Bruce, "Modern Homes at Roslyn Oxley9 Gallery", *Sydney Morning Herald*,
September 13 1996
Johnson, Anna, "Tuft Decisions...", *Australian Vogue*, March 1998
King, Natalie, "Displayed", *Art & Australia*, 32.3, Autumn, 1995
McKenzie, Robyn, "Monuments to Family History", *The Age*, 2 August 1995
Renton, Andrew, "The Problem is...", *Art and Cultural Difference*, A & D
Publication, London, 1995

MEYER VAISMAN

Born 1960, Caracas, Venezuela
Lives and works in Caracas, Venezuela and New York, USA

Selected solo exhibitions since 1993
1996 *Green on the Outside, Red on the Inside (My Parents' Closet)*, 303
        Gallery, New York
1995 *Private Property*, Espacio 204, Caracas
1994 *Turkeys*, Galerie Templon, Paris
1993 *Meyer Vaisman Obras Recientes*, Centro Cultural Consolidado, Caracas
        Biblioteca Luis Angel Arango, Bogotá, Colombia, Museo de Monterrey,
        Monterrey, Mexico (catalogue)

Selected group exhibitions since 1995
1998 *Figurative Sculpture*, Patrick Painter Gallery, Los Angeles, CA
        La Bienal del Barro, Museo Alejandro Otero, Caracas, Venezuela
        Sao Paulo Bienale, Sao Paulo, Brazil
1997 *No Place Like Home*, Walker Art Center, Minneapolis
1996 *Inklusion/Exklusion: Art in the Age of Postcolonialism and Global
        Migration*, Steirscher Herbst 96, Graz, Austria (catalogue)
        Interzones, Kunstforeningen, Copenhagen (catalogue)
        Everything that is Interesting is New, Athens School of Fine Arts (The
        Factory), Athens
1995 Museum of Modern Art, New York
        Space of Time, Center for Fine Arts, Miami
        Ars 95, Museum of Contemporary Art, Helsinki
        Border Crawl, Kukje Galley, Seoul (catalogue)

Selected bibliography
Ayerza, Josefina, "Global Art", *Flash Art*, May 1995
Brillembourg, Carlos, "Green on the Outside, Red on the Inside", artist's project
for *BOMB*, 1994
Decter, Joshua, "Stupidity as Destiny", *Flash Art*, October 1994
Fuenmayor, Jesus, "Venezia/Venezuela: A Project for Artforum", *Artforum*,
Summer 1995
Hollander, Kurt, "Contra la pered/Against the wall", *Poliester*, Spring 1996
Hollander, Kurt, "The Caracas Connection", *Art in America*, July 1994
Karmel, Pepe, *The New York Times*, April 12 1996
Ponce de Leon, Carolina, "Meyer Vaisman at 303", *Art in America*, October 1996
Vaisman, Meyer, "I want to be in America", *Parkett 39*, Spring 1994

CARRIE MAE WEEMS

Born 1953, Portland, Oregon, USA
Lives and works in New York, USA

Selected solo exhibitions since 1995

1998 Whitney Museum of American Art at Philip Morris, New York,
Biennial, Dakkar, Senegal
1997 Virginia Museum of Fine Arts, Richmond, VA
1996 *From Here I Saw What Happened and I Cried*, PPOW, New York & US tour
Carrie Mae Weems: The Kitchen Table Series, Contemporary Arts Museum,
Houston
1995 *Carrie Mae Weems Reacts to Hidden Witness*, J. Paul Getty Museum of
Art, Malibu
Projects 52, Museum of Modern Art, New York
Sea Islands Series, Africa Series, Sarah Moody Gallery of Art, University of
Alabama, Tuscaloosa & US Tour

Selected group exhibitions since 1996

1998 *Bearing Witness: Contemporary Works by African-American Artists*, Polk
Museum of Art, Lakeland, Florida and US tour
Tell Me a Story: Narration in Contemporary Painting and Photography,
Centre National d'Art Contemporain de Grenoble, Grenoble, France
1997-8 *Changing Spaces*, Detroit Institute of Art, Detroit, Michigan
1997 *Alternating Currents, The Johannesburg Biennial*, Johannesburg, South Africa
Four Decades, PPOW, New York
Original Visions: Women, Art and the Politics of Gender, Boston College
Museum of Art, Boston, MA
Dislocations, Rovaniemi Art Museum, Finland
*Inclusion/Exclusion: Art in the Age of Post Colonialism and Global
Migration*, Steirischer Herbst, Austria
1996 *Inside the Visible*, Institute of Contemporary Art, Boston, MA
Gender Beyond Memory, Tokyo Metropolitan Museum of Photography,
Tokyo, Japan

Selected bibliography

Galassi, Peter, *Pleasures and Terrors of Domestic Comfort*, MOMA, NY, 1996
Golden, Thelma, *Black Male, Representations of Masculinity in Contemporary American
Art*, Whitney Museum of American Art, New York, 1994
Powell, Richard J., *Black Art and Culture in the 20th Century*, Thames & Hudson,
London
Sarah Moody Gallery, University of Alabama, *In these Islands*, South Carolina,
Georgia, essays by Houston A. Baker Jr. and bell hooks, 1994
Soutter, Lucy, "By Any Means Necessary: Document and Fiction in the Work of
Carrie Mae Weems", *Art & The Home*, Art & Design Profile No. 51, 1996, pp.
70-5

RACHEL WHITEREAD

Born 1963, London
Lives and works in London

Selected solo exhibitions since 1993
1997 British Pavilion, Venice Biennale
1996 Karsten Schubert Ltd, London
   Sculptures, Luhring Augustine Gallery, New York
   Shedding Life, Tate Gallery, Liverpool
1995 *Sculptures*, British School in Rome
   Untitled (Floor), Karsten Schubert Ltd, London
1994 *Drawings*, Galerie Aurel Scheibler, Cologne
   Sculptures, Kunsthalle Basel; ICA Philadelphia & Boston
   Drawings, Luhring Augustine Gallery, New York
1993 Galerie Claire Burrus, Paris
   Sculptures, Museum of Contemporary Art, Chicago
   House, commissioned by Artangel Trust and Beck's
   Drawings, DAAD Galerie, Berlin

Selected group exhibitions since 1995
1998 *Wounds*, Moderna Museet, Stockholm
1997 *Skulpture Projekte*, Munster
   Sensation, Royal Academy of Arts, London
1996 *ACE! Arts Council Collection New Purchases*, UK Tour
   *Works on Paper from the Weltkunst Collection of British Art of the 80s
   and 90s*, Irish Museum of Modern Art, Dublin
1995 *Double Mixte: Generique 2*, Galerie Nationale du Jeu de Paume, Paris
   Ars '95, Museum of Contemporary Art and Finnish National Gallery,
   Helsinki
   Five Rooms, Anthony d'Offay Gallery, London
   Here & Now, Serpentine Gallery, London
   Brilliant: New Art from London, Walker Art Centre, Minneapolis
   Carnegie International 1995, Carnegie Museum of Art, Pittsburgh
   Istanbul Biennial, Instanbul Foundation for Culture and Arts, Turkey

Selected bibliography
Debbaut, Jan (ed.), *Rachel Whiteread: Sculptures*, ex. cat., Stedelijk Van
Abbemuseum, Windhaven, 1993
House, Phaidon Press Ltd, London, 1995
Kellein, Thomas (ed.), *Rachel Whiteread: Sculptures*, ex. cat., ICA Boston & ICA
Philadelphia
Parkett no. 42, 1994
Shedding Life, Tate Gallery, Liverpool, 1996

Claustrophobia - Inside and Outside

Education Programme

Ikon Gallery presents the work of living artists to its wide ranging audiences through a lively and innovative education programme that offers different ways of engaging and responding to the exhibitions.

As part of the regular "Look Who's Talking..." series of Saturday afternoon talks, Ikon has invited a wide range of people from a variety of disciplines to share their personal responses to and perspectives on Claustrophobia. Speakers include poet Roz Goddard, Chaz Mason, representing Shelter - the Housing Aid Charity, Dorothy Hobson, writer and lecturer in "Daytime Drama", a retail merchandiser from Habitat, Birmingham, Melanie Friend, exhibiting artist, Julian Holder, archiectural historian and Dr. Patricia Newell, Lecturer in Environmental Psychology at the University of Warwick.

Alongside children's workshops led by artists Permindar Kaur and Nina Saunders, a component of the schools programme includes pupils from St. George's C.E. school, Ladywood and St. Mary's C.E. school, Selly Oak acting as guides within the exhibition. The children have worked closely with the artists and curators, experiencing behind-the-scenes activities, before spending two weeks in the galleries as information guides.

The children greet visitors coming into the exhibition spaces, encouraging them to see Claustrophobia from a child's eye view. These informal tours stimulate conversations and discussions across all age groups and boost the children's confidence and enthusiasm to share ideas with a range of people including gallery staff.

In addition, poet Roz Goddard leads a series of relaxed and informal creative writing workshops. Inspired by the exhibition, the workshops act as a catalyst for people to develop their own prose, script writing and poetry. Rachel Whiteread's video documentary of the making of 'HOUSE' is also screened alongside the BBC documentary 'Date with an Artist' which featured Nina's Saunders' domestic commission and a documentary on "Womanhouse", the feminist collaborative intervention of 1972.

The education programme was devised and organised by curator Deborah Kermode and information assistants Nicola Bowen and Neil Jones.

Living the Waking World Asleep - an offsite project

As an adjunct to *The Silent Partner*, Permindar Kaur devised an intervention for a loft apartment in the vicinity of Brindleyplace, site of the new Ikon. For one month, the owner of the apartment lives around five institutional beds (reminiscent of steel framed prison or hospital beds). Visitors to the off-site installation encounter the beds in the kitchen, bathroom, living room and hallways, unsure of the reasons for these multiple private objects in public spaces.

RECOMMENDED READING

Exhibition catalogues

Art & The Home, Art & Design Profile, No. 51, 1996

Chambres d'amis, Museum van Hedendaagse Kunst, Ghent, 1986

Dirt & Domesticity: Constructions of the Feminine, Whitney Museum of American Art at Equitable Center, 1992

Division of Labour: Women's Work in Contemporary Art, The Bronx Museum of Arts, New York, 1996

Embedded Metaphor, Independent Curators Inc., New York, 1996

House Rules, assemblage: A Critical Journal of Architecture and Design Culture, MIT Press in association with the Wexner Center for the Arts, 1994

Il progretto domestico: Le casa dell'uomo archetipi e protipi, 17th Triennale Milano, 1986

No Place Like Home, Walker Art Center, Minneapolis, 1997

Pleasures and Terrors of Domestic Comfort, Museum of Modern Art, New York, 1991

Sense and Sensibility: Women Artists and Minimalism in the Nineties, Museum of Modern Art, New York, 1994

Within these Walls, Kettle's Yard, Cambridge, 1997

Bachelard, Gaston, *The Poetics of Space*, trans. Maria Jolas, Beacon Press, Boston, 1994

Bammer, Angelika, (ed.), "The Question of "Home", *new formations: A Journal of Culture/Theory/Politics*, No. 17, Summer 1992

Colomina, Beatriz, (ed.), *Sexuality & Space*, Princeton Papers on Architecture, New York, Princeton Architectural Press, 1992

French, Marilyn, *The Women's Room*, Sphere Books, 1977

Freud, Sigmund, "The Uncanny", *Standard Edition of the Complete Psychological Works*, trans. James Strachey, et. al., The Hogarth Press and Institute of Psycho-Analysis, 1953, vol. XV11

Gilman, Charlotte Perkins, *The Yellow Wallpaper*, Virago Press, 1996 (first published 1892)

Lewis, C.S., *The Lion, the Witch and the Wardrobe*, London, 1980

Massey, Doreen, *Space, Place and Gender*, Polity Press, 1994

Rybczynski, Witold, *Home: A Short History of an Idea*, New York, 1982

Reed, Christopher, (ed.), *Not at Home: The Suppression of Domesticity in Modern Art and Architecture*, Thames and Hudson, 1996

Scarry, Elaine, *The Body in Pain: The Making and Unmaking of the World*, Oxford University Press, 1985

Stewart, Susan, *On Longing: Narratives of the Miniature, the Gigantic, the Souvenir, the Collection*, Johns Hopkins, Baltimore, 1984

Vale, Brenda, *Prefabs: A History of the UK Temporary Housing Programme*, E & F N Spon, 1995

Vidler, Anthony, *The Architectural Uncanny: Essays in the Modern Unhomely*, MIT Press, 1992

Wood, Sarah, (ed.), "home and family", *Angelaki 2:1*, 1995

ACKNOWLEDGEMENTS

Lenders to the exhibition
Caldic Collectie, Rotterdam
Collection Lynn and Peter Harrison, California
Collection Eric Mellencamp, Seal Beach, California
Collection Hilarie and Mark Moore, Orange, California
National Museum of Photography, Film and Television, Bradford
Collection of Eileen and Peter Norton, Santa Monica
Collezione Re Rebaudengo Sandretto, Torino
Collection Brian & Kalli Rolfe, Melbourne
Tate Gallery, London (Purchased with assistance from the Patrons of New Art
through the Tate Gallery Foundation, 1993)
Private Collections in London, Melbourne and Connecticut

For their continued assistance and support for this project:
Alexander and Bonin, New York; Anthony d'Offay Gallery, London;
Bonakdar Jancou Gallery, New York; Lisson Gallery, London; London Projects,
London; Mark Moore Gallery, Santa Monica, California; PPOW, New York
Sean Kelly Gallery, New York; Tolarno Galleries, Melbourne
Aberystwyth Arts Centre; Cartwright Hall, Bradford; Centre for Visual Arts,
Cardif; Dundee Contemporary Arts; Mappin Art Gallery, Sheffield;
Middlesbrough Art Gallery
Hatice Abdullah, Camerawork, London; Pat & Tom Attenborrow; Avoncroft
Museum of Buildings, Bromsgrove; Catherine Bate (installation intern); Dr. Nigel
Buller; Natalie King, freelance curator (formerly Assistant Curator, Monash
University Gallery, Melbourne); Paul Miller, East Adriatic Team, Amnesty
International; Paul Taylor, Local Studies and History Department, Birmingham
Central Library; Steve Walker, Technical Services Officer, Housing Department,
Birmingham City Council

Artists' Acknowledgements
Carolyn Eskdale: Greg Creek; Melanie Friend: Arta Dedaj (translator of written
texts); Permindar Kaur: Nick Lister (construction of bed); Nina Saunders: Pete
Locker (artist/technician), John Discombe (engineering expertise), Hackney
Council Amenities for swing and swing structure, Publishers Allo Music/Chrysalis
for the use of "Forever", author Vlavianos-Constandinos, "Forever" by Englebert
Humperdinck courtesy of EMI Records

Published in June 1998 by Ikon Gallery to coincide with the exhibition
Claustrophobia at Ikon Gallery, 6 June to 2 August 1998.

1 Oozells Square, Brindleyplace, Birmingham B1 2HS
Tel: +00 44 121 248 0708 Fax: +00 44 121 248 0709
email: art@ikon-gallery.co.uk

Edited by Claire Doherty
Designed by Z3, Birmingham
Printed by Hill Shorter, West Bromwich
Distributed by Cornerhouse Publications, 70 Oxford Street, Manchester M1 5NH
Tel: +00 44 161 228 2463

ISBN 0 907594 58 1

Claustrophobia is supported by the Henry Moore Foundation and by the
Commonwealth Government through the Australia Council, its arts and funding
advisory body, with a research and development grant from the Arts Council of
England and Professional Development International Exchange Award from the
British Council in 1996 which enabled the selection of the Australian artists.

Ikon Gallery gratefully acknowledges financially assistance from the Arts Council
of England, Birmingham City Council and West Midlands Arts.
Registered charity no: 528892